KT-468-099

Streetwise

Stories from an Irish Prison

Edited by
Neville Thompson

MAINSTREAM
PUBLISHING

EDINBURGH AND LONDON

Reprinted 2007, 2008

Copyright © The Contributors, 2004
All rights reserved
The moral rights of the authors have been asserted

First published in Great Britain in 2004 by
MAINSTREAM PUBLISHING COMPANY (EDINBURGH) LTD
7 Albany Street
Edinburgh EH1 3UG

ISBN 9781840188738

No part of this book may be reproduced or transmitted in
any form or by any means without written permission from
the publisher, except by a reviewer who wishes to quote brief
passages in connection with a review written for insertion in
a newspaper, magazine or broadcast

The author has tried to clear all copyright permissions, but
where this has not been possible and amendments are
required, the publisher will be pleased to make any necessary
arrangements at the earliest opportunity

A catalogue record for this book is
available from the British Library

Typeset in Baskerville Book and New Courier

Printed in Great Britain by
Clays Ltd, St Ives plc

Contents

Contents

Marino Branch
Brainse Marglann Mhuirine
Tel. 8336297

Streetwise

Introduction

I first began working in Irish prisons in 2000. Linda Tynan, a teacher in Portlaoise prison at the time, had noticed that some of her students were reading my novels and asked me if I'd come in and give a talk. Visiting prisons was an all-new experience. I found myself in a room full of total strangers, and yet I felt that I knew half of them, as I'd seen their photos splashed across the Sunday papers.

As an author you get used to people asking the same questions over and over again. One of the most frequently asked, for me, was asked again on my first visit to the prison: 'Why hasn't your novel *Jackie Loves Johnser OK?* been made into a film?'

'Well, it's not as simple as that. Even a small-budget film costs millions.'

Quick as a flash one of the most infamous inmates answered, in a deadpan voice, 'Money, Nev, is not a problem.'

The whole room cracked up, me included. What this made me realise is that there is a great wealth of talented, entertaining people in prison.

Thanks to the initiative of Evelyn Conway, the chief librarian in prisons, to bring writing workshops into the prison libraries, I began working regularly within the

Leabharlanna Poibli Chathair Bhaile Átha Cliath
Dublin City Public Libraries

prisons. Time after time I was struck by the talent that I came across.

When myself and Bredha Sexton, head of drama in Midlands Prison, held auditions for *Sex, Lies and Butterflies*, the first play ever performed in Midlands, the response and depth of talent was so impressive that I had to go away and write in five extra characters. And yet, despite all this talent, no one seemed to be tapping into it.

The common perception of prisoners is that they are low life: uneducated wasters who all have a huge chip on their shoulders. Although there are a lot of prisoners who fit that description perfectly, there are a lot of people on the outside who fit that description perfectly too.

I would never consider myself to be a do-gooder – if I caught someone breaking into my home, I would happily throttle them and feel no remorse – and I know that people don't go to prison for being law-abiding citizens. However, within the prison community I have met people who I am glad to call friends. For these people, I'm prepared to go that extra mile, and I know that they would do the same for me.

None of the writers featured in this book had ever attended a workshop before now. When this project was mentioned, most of them thought they would never manage to write more than a page. But they were wrong. Many of them discovered that they had the necessary level of commitment to get their stories onto paper. For some, it was the first time in their lives they had seen something through to the end.

When we first discussed the possibility of doing this book it was their suggestion, not mine, that any money we made from royalties should go to charity. The authors have chosen four children's hospitals in Ireland – Our Lady's Hospital for Sick Children, Crumlin Road, Dublin; Temple Street

Children's Hospital, Dublin; Cork University Hospital, Children's Unit; Limerick Regional Hospital, Children's Unit – and I hope we make a fortune for them.

The works featured in this book are faction – more fact than fiction. Because of this, I sincerely believe that this book is a true representation of life on their side of the fence. All names are changed to protect those people involved and their families.

Allowing these writers a voice doesn't make them any less a criminal, but I hope it proves they are much more than a statistic too. What I have tried to do as editor of this book is to help make these great stories come to life. I truly feel that they represent a great mix of writers and the broad spectrum of lives within the prison system.

As a group, the writers and I would like to thank Mainstream Publishing for this opportunity and for the great care they have taken with this book. I personally wish to thank Sean Wynne, head of education, and John O'Sullivan, Governor of Midlands Prison, for their support in this project. Finally, I want to acknowledge the enormous work that my wife, Jean, put into editing the text. Without her, this book would not have seen the light of day.

Neville Thompson

Mucka, a Life - by Mucka

I had always been fascinated with school, ever since that first day when my mother said I could make my own way there . . . under one condition, that I wasn't to be late. Her words always stuck in my brain, I would never be late.

Not only would I never be late, I'd be first at the gate every morning, come rain or shine, with my two sandwiches that I ate for the morning break.

We had two breaks during our school day: a small break at 11.00 a.m. and the big lunch break from 12.30 p.m. until 1.30 p.m. Most of the other children didn't arrive back from lunch until 1.45 p.m., but not me. No, I would be back at the gate at 1.30 p.m. on the dot.

I always liked to be first in the classroom to make sure I got the seat straight in front of the teacher's desk. I'd sit there thinking, 'I'm more important than the rest of the class. In fact, never mind the class, I'm more special than the whole of the school put together.'

The year of my first communion, Master Taylor told the whole class that I had a special gift for learning, as I'd learnt off all of the Holy Communion prayers, having heard them only once.

He patted me on the head. 'You must have been a priest in a past life.'

My reward was to give out all the prayer books and to gather them in again at the end of the class. I could see the envious glances of the others as I handed them out.

On Holy Communion day I led the class up the aisle to the altar. I got my Holy Communion before everybody else, and as Master Taylor looked on he said I would definitely go places with my determination always to be first.

Even during the summer holidays I'd arrive at the locked school gate and stand there and offer up my prayers for our education. And on the days when the gate was open I would go all the way to the school door and offer my prayers from there.

One morning when I arrived to give my daily offering I saw that the door was open. I rushed in, my heart in my mouth, full of excitement. I ran straight to my classroom. All my prayers had been answered, for the classroom door was ajar. I rushed inside. 'Hello, Mr Taylor . . .'

But it wasn't Mr Taylor, it was Mrs White, the cleaning woman, and she was howling like a banshee telling me that I had put the heart across her. 'Who are you? What are you doing here, you little pup?'

Before I could answer she started shouting at me, her arms flaying, suds flying everywhere.

'I said what are you doing here? Who let you in? You have no right to be here.'

With tears streaming down my face I told her I was sorry.

'What's your name?'

Like a prisoner of war, I told her my name and class.

'Well, wait till I see Master Taylor. I'll be telling him about your carry on. Now be off with you before I call the guards.'

I was out the door like a shot, through the school grounds and out the gate. Without looking left or right, I ran straight out onto the road. Suddenly I was flying ten feet in the air, landing on my skull to the sound of a car braking.

I could feel the blood running down my face. The driver of the car was kneeling at my side, apologising to the gathering crowd, telling them that he hadn't even seen me coming.

He was asking me where I lived and if my parents were at home. When I told him there was nobody in my house he said he'd take me to the hospital himself. He drove off with me in the passenger seat. As soon as we were out of sight of all the prying eyes, the man stopped the car. He got out and dragged me out of the car. I was screaming in pain. He dumped me in someone's front garden and took off. I was only brought to hospital after the man of the house rang the guards to tell them there was a vagrant in his garden.

In the hospital the nurse tried to get information out of me but all I could do was cry for me mammy.

'Where is your mother?'

'At home.'

'Where is home?'

'Near the school.'

'What school?'

'Plunkett Street.'

'What number?

'61.'

'And does your mother have a telephone?'

Another nurse who was standing nearby laughed.

'Don't be stupid. No house up in Ballypheane has a telephone.'

Mammy arrived at the hospital courtesy of the local *gardai* who had called at the house to tell her about my accident. A few hours later I was discharged and Mammy brought me home on the bus. I slept on the sofa for a week so Mammy could keep an eye on me.

Then the day I had been praying for arrived . . . the day I could go back to school.

I was first in line standing outside Mr Taylor's class. I was sure he'd be delighted to see me.

'Welcome back, Michael, what are you doing here?'

'I'm OK now, Mr Taylor, so I've come back to school.'

'I'm sure you are but you shouldn't be here. You're in Mrs Morris's class now, not mine.'

He must have seen the tears in my eyes. He put his hand on my shoulder. 'You're a big lad now, Michael, you've moved up to room three. Keep up the good work, Michael.'

I felt a little better now that Mr Taylor had complimented me. Maybe room three wouldn't be too bad.

When I reached room three, all the lads were at their desks. Mrs Morris spoke without looking at me.

'Take a seat.'

I didn't move. She turned around.

'Take a seat at the back of the room.'

'Sorry, Miss, but do you think I could sit up the front?'

She looked me up and down.

'You cheeky pup. Just do as you're told and stop disturbing my class.'

She watched me as I made my way sulkily toward the back of the room.

'I can see I'm going to have trouble with you . . . what's your name?'

'Michael, Miss.'

'Well, Michael, sit down and be quiet. I don't want to hear a word out of you for the rest of term.'

The adrenalin that had been rushing through my body faded, and from that moment on nothing ever went right for me again.

By eleven o'clock, I had my first fight ever. I saw the boy who had taken my seat in Mr Taylor's class. I ran over and grabbed him by his hair and sank my teeth into his cheek. I was growling like a dog and shaking my head from side to side. Blood was running down my chin and the boy was crying like a baby, but I held on. Teachers ran over and tried to separate us, but I hung on like a terrier dog, trying to snap the boy in two. One of the teachers was sitting on me but my blood was surging through my veins, giving me superhuman strength. I was wild with rage. I heard someone say that there was froth coming from my mouth. Mr Roche, the headmaster, came bursting onto the scene.

'What the hell is going on here?'

The teacher sitting on top of me tried to explain as I wriggled and screamed to be released.

'Let the boy up,' said Mr Roche.

'But . . .'

'No buts, let him up. There's no need to flatten the poor crater.'

The minute the teacher took some of his weight off me I was up and running, weaving to avoid colliding with the teachers. As I ran for the gate, voices in the background screamed at me to stop. I was on the road and heading . . . I don't know where, when suddenly I was sailing through the air. As my body thumped to the ground, I heard a car skidding to a halt . . . people screamed . . . and then blackness.

When I woke up I was back in the hospital. My leg was broken in a few places and I was concussed again. The only visitor I had was a social worker who said my mother didn't want me at home because I only disturbed my sisters and kid brother. I asked her what she meant.

'Your mother says you're like a wild animal and that you attacked her. She says there's evil in your eyes and she doesn't want you near her home until your father gets out of prison.'

Jaysus, and there was me thinking my aul fella was on the oil rigs and not due back for another four years.

'I'm only eight years old, where am I supposed to go?'

The tears are rolling down my cheeks as she stands there with her big social worker's smile, telling me I'll find out soon enough. I wanted to jump out of the bed and run, but my leg wouldn't move.

I was driven in a minibus to the biggest house I'd ever seen. The woman of the house came out and, taking one look at me, said that the first thing I'd be getting was a good wash.

Against my wishes, she wrapped my plastered leg in a black bag and threw buckets of cold water over me. I hated them all and decided that I wouldn't speak a word to them, ever! And I didn't.

One month later I was brought to the hospital to have my plaster of Paris removed. I had to wait for an X-ray to see if the joint had healed. Still not speaking, I pointed to the zip of my trousers, indicating that I needed to go to the toilet. I was escorted to the toilet but allowed into the cubicle alone. Once the door was locked I was up on the cistern, out the big window and across the car park. I made my way to my uncle's scrapyard. When he saw me, he looked amazed.

'I thought the Christian Brothers had you!'

'Look, Leo, I ran away from the hospital.'

'Are you off your rocker coming into my yard? Did anyone see you, lad?'

'No, they're still waiting outside the toilet for me.'

He grabbed me by the scruff of the neck.

'Get into the back shed before you get this place shut down on me.'

Ducking like a soldier in the trenches, I made my way to the shed. Leo shut the gate and joined me in the shed.

'What the hell are you up to?'

'I'm not going back, Leo. Nearly five weeks and no one visited me. And I don't even know why I'm there in the first place, I done nothing wrong.'

'Nothing wrong? You went crazy, biting everyone, attacking teachers, running at cars. Sure, your mother is shocked by your carry on and is afraid of her life of you.'

'Leo, Leo, I don't remember any of that. There was a red-headed lad picking on me in the schoolyard and I punched him and fell on top of him. That's all I did, I swear. Sure, I wouldn't lie to you. There's no way I'm going back to the Christian Brothers. Remember Daddy used to talk about the way they treated him in Letterfrack? Leo, if I have to go back there, I'll run away again.'

'I know that you will. Is your mother sober or drunk these days?'

'Well, she usually has a few bottles after she's been up to see my da. She says she can't sleep after seeing him.'

'I can't talk to that woman when she's on the bottle.' He thought for a minute. 'I'll get Dennis to take you to his place in Blackhall until I can get a better idea of what to do.'

'Do you think he'll take me?'

'There's no doubt he'll take you but only until we can get one of your uncles in England to take you. But I'm warning you now, you'll have to stay inside at all times. You can't even go out for a shite until it's dark. Get that into your thick head.'

I nodded in agreement. One hour later I was hiding in the back seat of Leo's van on my way to Blackhall. Leo stopped the van outside a shop.

'Go in and get me twenty Major.'

'But you said I was to stay out of sight.'

'Just do what you're told!'

I hobbled towards the shop. I looked in the window and could see the blue shirt of a shade (a *garda*). I turned towards the van and indicated to Leo but he just waved me in. As soon as I opened the shop door the shade was on me, telling me he knew who I was and dragging me out the side door. I couldn't scream for help or he'd have been on to Leo too. He brought me to the police station and, as I ate a fish and chip dinner, I was asked the same question over and over again: why had I run away?

The policeman told me I'd be appearing in the children's court the following day. The next morning, on the way to the court, the squad car stopped at my mother's house. The front door was open and I could hear her singing at the top of her voice. This could only mean one thing: she'd got her hands on a bottle of Bushmills.

The shade knocked on the door and walked in, as if it was a public house.

'Get out of here, you bastard. What gives you the right to come into my house uninvited? May you rot in hell, the lot of yous.'

'We have your son in the car and he's up in the District Court at 2.30 p.m. this afternoon, ma'am.'

'May God curse you and may the fever melt you, you lying puny bastard! You have no son of mine.'

'He's in the back of the squad car and he's on his way to court. You can come with us but you'll have to sober up and behave in a proper manner.'

From the back of the squad car I saw the shade duck and the empty whiskey bottle smash against the wall. He ran back to the car.

'I don't think your mother will be in court today unless she gets arrested herself.'

The judge sentenced me to twenty-eight days in the custody of some foster parents in East Cork. East Cork was fifteen miles away, but being so young it felt like I was on my way to the other side of Ireland.

The house was the nicest I'd ever been in. The woman told me they had three toilets.

'Well yous must shite a lot, if yous need three toilets,' I told her.

She leaned towards me. 'I think you should go to your room. My children are not used to that kind of language.'

I limped to my bedroom, where I lay on the bed and cried.

A short time later the woman came into the room and asked me if I was OK. I found myself telling her the story of my broken leg.

'Well, if you can keep a civil tongue in your head, you can go down and play with my children and perhaps Benjy might give you a bar of chocolate.'

I walked down the hall and into the recreation room that looked out over the fields. I'll be across those fields as soon as I can run, I thought.

There were two boys in the room.

'Which one of yous is Benjy?'

'I am,' said the boy playing with a garage. 'Do you want to play with me?'

'No. I want chocolate.'

'But we'll be having dinner shortly.'

'Your ma said you'd give me chocolate.'

'Daddy will be very cross if you eat sweets before dinner.'

'Fuck him.'

Benjy put his hand over his mouth in shock. 'You're not allowed to use language like that in this house.'

'Just get me the chocolate, now!'

Benjy ran from the room and came back seconds later, chocolate in hand. Ignoring him, I stuffed the bar into my mouth and stared out the window.

The woman of the house appeared at the door and called me by my name. The cheek of her. Only my mammy called me by my proper name, and what was even stranger was that she was telling me it was time for my bath and some new clothes.

'You're joking. I always have my bath on Saturday night and change my clothes then whether I need to or not.'

'Let's not have any arguments now. OK? You're getting

out of those clothes and having a bath. My husband is due home at any minute and I want you to be clean and fresh when he sees you.'

I stood my ground and continued to stare out of the window. A car came up the driveway; the man of the house was home. My heart was racing as I watched him get out and approach the house; I had never seen such a pig belly on a man before. The family scattered. I could hear low whispering from the woman and Benjy as they stood in the hallway but couldn't work out what was being said.

The floorboards creaked as he entered the room.

'All right young man, bath . . . now!' he said.

I shook my head. 'No.'

'Right, follow me to the bedroom. We're going to have a little man-to-man.'

I didn't move. His face turned a funny colour as he continued.

'I'll give you time to think about your actions. Stay right where you are until I return.'

He left the room. I stood where I was for what seemed like ages. My leg was killing me. It wasn't until it was getting dark that I sat down. The door opened.

'You need to be taught a lesson. Stand up and remove your clothes.'

I didn't move. His hand caught me by the collar of my jumper and he dragged me to the bathroom. He tore off my trousers, making me scream in pain as he dragged them over my broken shin. Leaving the rest of my clothes on, he threw me into the cold bath.

'Take off those clothes and wash yourself. No one goes against my wishes in my house.'

I took off my shoes and threw them at him.

'Fuck you. I hate you! And when my daddy gets out of prison he'll kick the shite out of you!'

I was ranting and raving so much that I didn't notice his hand until it landed flat on the side of my face.

'If you don't want more of the same, you'll get those clothes off and wash yourself.'

I did what I was told. He came back to the bathroom with clean clothes.

'Get them clothes on and join us for a bite to eat.'

When he was gone I took my wet clothes out of the linen basket and, putting them on, walked out to the kitchen. It was the final straw. He ran straight at me, ripping the clothes off my back leaving me stark naked. He dragged me out into the garden and turned the hose on me.

'I told you to put on clean clothes, didn't I?'

'No! You told me to put on clothes.'

'You know what I meant.'

'I'm only a child, I can't read your mind.'

He looked at me as though he was deciding whether to kill me or not. From the door, his wife shouted for him to stop. Through clenched teeth he told me to go to my room, dry myself and put on clean dry clothes. When I was dressed I was to go to the kitchen and eat every mouthful of the food on my plate.

I wolfed down the food. This was an evil man and I wasn't going to upset him again. I could feel the heat spreading over my body. The more I ate, the hotter I became. Sweat ran down my back and my clothes felt as though they were suffocating me. The room started to spin and I couldn't breathe. I felt the chair go from under me and the woman started to scream.

When I woke up in the hospital, a kind doctor was telling me I was going to be fine. They had pumped my stomach and it seemed that I had an allergy to certain types of food.

'Mr Doctor, I knew that. My mammy told me. But I was so afraid that if I didn't eat my food that man and his wife would continue to hurt me.'

'Are you telling me that those people in the waiting room are not your mother and father?'

'No, my mammy's at home and my daddy's in jail. The courts put me in the custody of those people today. Since that man came home from work, I've been bullied, stripped naked, and hosed down in the freezing cold yard just because I put the wrong clothes on. Please don't let them take me back to their house cause he'll fucking kill me.'

The doctor left the room and a woman in a navy suit entered. She had that social-worker attitude about her. After I had finished telling her all that had happened to me, she told me not to worry – I'd be staying in the hospital for a few days and the authorities would deal with the foster parents. I was moved onto the children's ward and the minute my head touched the pillow I fell asleep.

When I woke up, my mammy was sitting by the side of my bed, stone cold sober. She promised that she'd never drink again and that she'd look after me as if I was the Crown Jewels. She said that she'd put a curse on the foster parents that their hands would fall off if they ever raised them to another child again.

When I left the hospital, I was the happiest boy on earth.

Four weeks later I came skipping down the road to the sound of Mammy singing at the top of her voice.

'Mammy, you promised. You promised you'd never touch another drop!'

'Whished, you moggy boy. I'm only celebrating the fact that the foster parent lad has had an order of supervision put on him.'

'But, Mammy, the neighbours will have the shades on you if you don't stop all that singing.'

'They will not. I'll just finish this bottle and go to my bed.'

'And what about my tea and my lunch for school?'

'Take yourself away to the chipper. Get a quarter of corned beef, bread and butter and a pack of Woodbines in the shop on your way back.'

As I took off across the fields, my heart was low. I knew that Mammy wouldn't stop drinking and pretty soon the shades would be back banging on our door. I knew that, despite Mammy's best intentions, nothing would ever change.

I made a short cut through the school, running along the school sheds to save time. From my vantage point I could see into Mrs Cutter's classroom and there in the open drawer of Mrs Cutter's desk I could see the box that held the money for the schoolbooks.

The adrenalin started to flow. I knew I was doing myself wrong but the temptation was too much . . . and besides, now that Mammy was back drinking, I knew things were never going to be the same again.

Stolen Years - by Fatboy

1972 - where it all began

From the minute I drew my first breath, I knew the path my life would take. Don't ask me how I knew . . . I just did.

1978 - the first time

I was five years old and was standing at the back of the local supermarket when I got a feeling I had never felt before. I looked up and down the shop, no one was watching . . . I could just take something and walk out . . . no one would notice. My heart was pounding in my chest. I grabbed a packet of biscuits, hid them under my jacket and walked straight out the door . . . freedom!

I felt great. I ran to find my friends. I couldn't wait to tell them all about my big adventure. The funny thing is, I didn't even like the biscuits I'd stolen, but that didn't matter. What mattered was that I did it. I had found my calling.

I always hated school. From the first day I entered the classroom, I knew I was going to hate it. And I also hated the teacher, who hated me in return. Back then, teachers could do what they liked to kids. They could batter you for no apparent reason and get away with it. And if you dared to complain to your parents, they battered you too. So I never complained, I just kept myself to myself.

1980 – the move

When I heard we were moving to a new housing estate in Tallaght, I was delighted. But the delight didn't last long. I made a lot of new friends when I moved to Tallaght, but, like me, they were bored shitless. We got fed up playing kids' games so we started to make our own entertainment.

Our estate was a bit like a building site, with lots of new houses that hadn't been finished yet. So, whenever we got the chance, we'd get onto the site and rob it blind. No matter what you robbed, you could sell it on our estate. There was always someone willing to pay good money for anything they thought was a bargain. Sometimes the adults would come robbing with us. It was great going robbing with the adults because we knew that they would look after us no matter what shit hit the fan.

1981 to 1984 – gangs and gas

By 1981, I only went to school when I felt like it. School was fucking stupid and there was no money to be made out of going to school. Besides, I was part of a gang now: me, Jay, Anto, Tommy and Willie. We were all as mad as each other and none of us went to school regularly.

One Wednesday we decided to go to school. The reason for this was that it was raining and we had nothing better to do. Besides, Wednesday was currant-bun day and we all loved currant-buns. We were in Mrs Harte's class. She was an ugly cunt who wore big round glasses like Deirdre Barlow from *Coronation Street* and we hated her. Anyway, on this particular day we decided to play a trick on her. Like I said, Wednesday was currant-bun day and we always tried to sky a few extra buns to have for ourselves later. On this particular Wednesday we only managed to sky one bun. Jay and Willie took the bun out to the jacks, split it in half, shit in it then squashed it back together. They walked back into the class and dropped the bun onto Harte's chair. No sooner had they sat down, when in walks Mr Kelly. Kelly was a right bastard who hated us. Anyway, the thick fucker came in and without saying a word he started rooting in Mrs Harte's drawers. Rumour had it that he was always rooting in her drawers! As he was rooting, he sat down, and the bun was squashed into his trousers. When he'd found what he was rooting for, he went back to his own class.

Within seconds we heard a shout from next door and all the kids laughing. Kelly came flying back into the room . . . fuming.

'Who did this?'

He turned around and we all saw the shit stains on the arse of his trousers. The whole class were pissing themselves laughing. Mrs Harte was shouting that we were all on detention until they found out who did this. Of course, Kelly sussed immediately who the culprits were, and me and the rest of my gang were frogmarched to the headmaster's office. We got such a hiding we couldn't sit for a week, but it was worth it.

Three years later and it's a new school and a new buzz . . . sniffing. We sniffed anything we could get our hands on: glue, gas, petrol, shoe polish . . . anything. One day, when we were walking down the road, we spotted a cylinder of gas on the back of the road workers' van. There was no one around, and before you could say 'Calor Kosangas' we had the cylinder off the van and into the Backers (the Backers was what we called the field at the back of our estate).

Once we'd reached the Backers, we started fighting over who would go first. As usual, Jay ended up going first because we all knew he'd kick our arses if he didn't. I didn't give a shite who went first, we had enough gas to last us a month!

The buzz was amazing. We were all pissing ourselves

laughing, at nothing. When you stop sniffing, your feet feel like they're wet and you get a buzzing sensation that starts in your legs and travels through your whole body until whack – it reaches your brain. You end up walking like a zombie. It only lasts a few seconds but it's the weirdest feeling ever.

After a while, Tommy started going on a mad one. I swear, he was acting like a madman. He said that he'd seen the devil and that the devil had ordered him to strip off all his clothes. He was running around the field bollock-naked, talking to the devil. At first we thought it was funny, but then it started to freak us out. Eventually we got him dressed and we all got the fuck out of there.

When we got back to our estate, Tommy said that he still felt shite. He was finding it hard to breathe, and Jay told him he was a funny colour. Next thing I know, he's lying on the ground having a seizure. His eyes are rolling around in his head and we're all screaming. While Willie was trying to resuscitate him, I legged it to his ma's house, but it was too late.

Tommy died at the grand old age of twelve.

1984 – cars, cars, cars

A new plague had hit Dublin . . . joyriding.

Cars would come screeching onto our estate doing handbrake turns and flashing their lights for hours on end and no one would dare to do a thing about it. We were the people who ran our estate and if some thick copper was stupid enough to interfere he'd be either stoned, rammed or petrol-bombed. Not that that ever stopped them! At that time Tallaght only had eight policemen. So whatever estate reported the first stolen car was the one they all headed to, leaving the rest of us to run wild.

By 1986, joyriding was still a serious problem, but drugs were becoming just as serious. Our estate was like Beirut.

Cars were being burnt out every night of the week and any derelict house became an inferno.

By 1995, you could get any drug you fancied, no problem. Heroin, coke, meths, napps. If it had a name, it had a price. 1995 was a real fucked-up year. The buses wouldn't drive into our estate after seven in the evening. One in every three houses had been broken into and the Sinn Feiners were rallying the people to march on drug-pushers' houses.

TADD (Tallaght Against Drug-Dealers) started putting posters up naming and shaming the pushers, and when TADD marched on the pushers' houses journalists always accompanied them. Our estate even featured on Sky News!

1998 - the end of the summer

It was 21 September 1998. The sun was splitting the sky and I was pointing the garden wall for my ma. Out of nowhere came a BMW. I knew it was stolen because Joe was in the driver's seat and he couldn't afford a BMW. He asked me if I wanted to go for a spin to discuss a job he had on. I said no, because I wanted to finish pointing the wall for my ma. He fucked off and I went in to have my tea. As I was eating, a newsflash came on the radio. The presenter was saying that a stolen car had been involved in a bad crash on the north side of the city. Even though I knew Joe had only been gone ten minutes, I had a bad feeling in my stomach.

Two hours later and the cops were outside Stevie's house. Stevie was only nineteen but he was a great fucking skin, mad as a hatter. He had been travelling in robbed cars since he was three years old. His mother came out of the house screaming. Telling us that Stevie was in the stolen car.

Seven days later, they turned off his life-support machine. It was just as well, really, because his brain would have been mush. Stevie's death hit me hard. I had really liked Stevie, and part of me wished it had been me instead of him who had died.

After the funeral, I went home and sat staring at the television. I was stoned out of my head on heroin. I needed something for my broken heart. As I sat staring at the telly, *Crimewatch* came on and there, as large as life, on the CCTV was my little homeboy, Stevie. It brought a smile to my face. The fuckers would never get him now.

I closed my eyes and prayed for my Stevie.

1979–1998. Rest in peace, SRF.

Shit Happens – by D.M.

I'm sitting in the rec in the Midlands prison.

The correct name is the Recreation Hall but that's a load of shite. I mean, what recreation ever goes on in here? There's a table tennis table without a net and a pool table that us Dubs never get a chance to use because the culchies are always on it. So, all that's left for us to do is sit around, smoking joints and exchanging stupid war stories.

BA was telling another one of his fucking stupid stories about Tasha flashing her tash, when a screw called me for a visit.

'Who's on the visit?' I asked as we walked towards the visitors' room.

'Your mother.'

That's all he said . . . cunt. No explanation. No nothing.

I was worried. I mean, my ma hadn't said she'd be coming up today and Ma never came on a visit without telling me. After all, she has the two babies to look after, so for her to have to organise someone to come in and mind those two little terrors, it had to be something serious.

I'm sitting in the visiting room and a million things are going through my brain. What the fuck's happening now? I hoped it wasn't Gary. Gary is my youngest brother and he was starting to get a bit wild and was hanging around with

31

the wrong crowd. A 'mini-me', just like Austin fucking Powers.

When I see Ma coming through the door, my worst fears are realised; Ma is crying.

Ma never cries. Well, not in front of screws she doesn't. She wouldn't give them the satisfaction of seeing her upset. And she knew that some of these bastards would take great pleasure in slagging me about it later.

Ma is a great woman, real strong and proud. And it takes a lot for her to show emotion. Ma hated upsetting us. As she'd say, it was all right for her because she was going back home but it was unfair on us having to go back to our cells. There are six boys in our family and four of us are locked up at the moment. Can you believe it – four out of six!

There were lots of visits taking place in the visiting room, but the minute the lads saw Ma coming in, the place went quiet. They knew by the look of her that something terrible had happened. A shiver ran up my spine. All I could think was that someone must be dead. But what was really freaking me was the screw standing on either side of me. Why couldn't they just fuck off and let me have a private visit?

It was obvious I was going to hear some seriously bad shit, and it was going to be announced to the whole fucking room. By the time I got back to me cell, every fucker in the prison would know my business.

I looked at the two screws, Bobble Jaws (because he had two big lumps like golf balls in his mouth) and Mars ('cause he's a dirt-bird spacer). They were sniggering to each other. I wanted to deck the two of them. It really crushed me to see the way they were treating this beautiful, energetic woman who was my ma. I wanted to smash their thick heads together and knock that stupid smirk off their evil faces. That would be great, wouldn't it? Me smashing the two fuckers up and Ma having to watch me being carted off, aeroplane-style, to the strip cell.

I reached out to touch her. I wanted to comfort her, to let her know it would all be OK. We'd get through this like we always did. After all, we were Marshes.

'Sit down, Marsh . . . you know the story . . . no physical contact.'

I was freaking. I mumbled something about them being thick culchie scumbags, but I knew I had to sit down or the visit would be terminated. That's all I'd fucking need. I watched Ma sobbing her heart out. After a few minutes and a little coaxing from me, she calmed down and started to explain what had happened.

'I got a phone call from Mountjoy this morning, David.'

'The Joy? What did they want?'

'They told me that Anto and Ned . . .'

'What about them . . . what did they tell you?'

'They're in the Mater.'

'The Mater! What for?'

As if I needed to ask. Everyone knew what two prisoners going to the Mater Hospital meant, but I didn't say anything. I wanted her to tell me.

'They OD'd.'

I didn't need to ask what they'd overdosed on. I already knew. Heroin was the drug of choice in the Marsh clan, and it wouldn't take a genius to work out how it had happened. Anto would have got some gear brought in on a visit and they'd have gone back to the cell to cook up. I knew they only had one works but us Marshes are great at sharing. So, Ned would have banged up first, seeing as he's the oldest, but he'd OD'd. Now Anto had two options. One: big brother is dying so he can hit the red light and get him help. If he hits the red light, the screws will come running and big brother will be saved, but the screws would find the gear. They'd pad him and, worse of all, he wouldn't get his own hit. Two: Anto can bang up himself, and when he's sure the drug is well and truly in the vein, he can then hit the red light. Anto chose option two. And as the screws reacted to the red light (red light spells danger, as Billy Ocean once sang), he OD'd too. The screws would have looked through the spyhole and seen two blue little boys.

I never realised the effect that our drug-taking had on my mother until now. It sounds silly, I know, but when you're involved in drug-taking, that's the only thing that matters – getting your hit. I knew if I had been with Anto and Ned, I'd have done the same thing. I wouldn't have given it a second thought. Drugs first . . . and everything else comes second.

Ma thought that once we'd been locked up we'd have a real chance to get clean and go back to being her boys again. People are so naive. They really believe all that shite about prison being a great place to get help and reform. The one thing that no one believes is that prison is a great place to get gear! Now, you don't always get the gear you want but you can still get it. One of the only problems with taking drugs in prison is the shortage of works, with the result that works have to be shared and you end up shooting up with a blunt works that has been passed down the landing. It's like playing Russian roulette, as you haven't a clue who's got HIV and who hasn't. But none of that really matters, because, like I say, drugs first.

What a disappointment we must be to Ma. A family of boys and all of us addicts! We were real selfish bastards putting Ma and Da through this. But the truth of the matter is that being a selfish bastard comes with the territory. Drug addicts don't think about their families, we don't think about the people we rob . . . for fuck sake, we don't even think about ourselves! All we think about is the next fix; remember the golden rule: drugs first.

And the minute the needle hits the vein, all that matters is the next fix. You don't even give yourself time to fully appreciate the score you've just had, before wham, you're thinking about the next fix and panicking in case you can't get enough money for a decent one. That's when the shakes start, the sweating, the paranoia. They say it only takes one addict to destroy a community. Poor Ma, she had a house full of them.

Ma was crying and apologising, saying what a lousy mother she was. Saying how she should have done better. I stopped her.

'No, Ma, you're not to blame. You were never to blame.'

I grew up in the flats. And before you all go jumping to conclusions and thinking, 'Ah, that explains everything,' let me tell you that our childhood was brilliant.

The flats were a brilliant place to grow up in. It's like people say about old Dublin . . . nobody ever had to lock their doors, we were like one big family. Sure, people fell out, just like families do, but if you were playing in a mate's flat his ma would feed you with her own kids and think nothing of it.

It was like a big holiday camp . . . like being in Butlins 365 days of the year. There was always something happening, loads to do. I used to feel sorry for anyone who didn't come from our flats. I loved getting up in the morning and couldn't wait to get out to play. At night, Ma would have to drag us in because we were having that much fun we didn't want it to end.

Da never missed a day's work in his life. And Ma worked nightshifts in a hospital to make ends meet. Not that we knew anything about that. We never wanted for anything. Our birthdays were filled with cakes and cards and presents, and when Santa visited our flat at Christmas he left everything we had asked for . . . and more.

35

Then Dublin started changing.

The older boys had found something new to entertain themselves with. At night, I'd lie in my bed and hear them exchanging stories about robbing, and it sounded so exciting that I wanted to go with them. I began to dream of robbing cars and breaking into houses. The Marshes! Ireland's very own James gang!

One evening I was watching Homer chasing Bart across the Simpsons' sitting room when there was a knock on our door. It was unusual to hear a knock, no one in the flats ever knocked, they didn't have to, the door was always open and they'd just shout in. The other thing that was unusual was Da went out and answered the door himself. Da never answered the door.

I could hear Da's voice. He sounded defensive, like he was talking to the television licence man or something.

'Yes, I'm Mr Marsh.'

I couldn't make out what the other voice was saying. Culchie voices are always difficult to understand, but I knew by the way Da was talking that the shit had hit the fan.

'Yes, Anto and Ned are my sons . . ?'

'Stolen car? Ah, no, there must be some mistake.'

Then nothing . . . silence.

I jumped up to the window and watched as Da and two policemen walked out to the squad car. I could just make out the two boys in the car. There was no mistake, it was them all right.

Da said he would agree to have them released into his custody. As soon as the boys got out of the squad car, they legged it past Da and into the house.

They stood in the middle of the sitting room. I'd never seen them looking so scared before. Usually one of them would be laughing and joking but not this time. Da went berserk! He was shouting and roaring about the shame they had brought on the family. He took off his belt and thrashed them until he couldn't raise his arm any more. My battered and bruised brothers swore they'd never rob again.

And they didn't . . . for about a week.

Over the next few months, the same scene was played over and over again in our sitting room, and before we knew where we were, the boys were sent to Saint Patrick's Detention Centre for Young Offenders for two years. I was twelve years old at the time and, despite my mother's tears and my father's ranting, it all seemed pretty cool to me.

When word of the sentence got around the flats . . . my two brothers were heroes! All my mates wanted to hear about their exploits and I was cool by association. Even some of the older boys wanted to hang out with me.

In an effort to try to deter me from a life of crime, Ma and Da brought me up to visit the boys. But I wasn't deterred, all I saw was Ned and Anto laughing and joking and making new friends. They seemed to be having the time of their lives. They'd look at me and try to look sincere when telling me never to get involved in crime, but I knew they didn't mean it.

When we got outside, Ma looked at me with tears in her eyes and made me swear that I would never rob. As I swore to her, I crossed my fingers behind my back so I knew my promise didn't count. She smiled down at me. As we made our way home, she talked about getting Mr Harris, the local photographer, to take a family picture.

'A family portrait. Now, wouldn't that be nice?'

The day the boys were due to be released, we all headed up to collect them. Ma was so happy that even the screw shouting that he'd see them again soon (and rubbing my head, telling me he bet he'd see me too) didn't dampen our day.

When we got home we had a big party, and we all had a drink to toast the boys.

'To no more robbing.'

Everyone held their drinks aloft and shouted, 'No more robbing.'

Ma hugged Anto. Behind her back, he looked at me and winked, and held up his crossed fingers.

Ma announced her plans for the family portrait and everyone said it was a great idea. Before she had a chance to arrange it, though, Anto was back in prison.

It was around this time that I started taking an interest in spelling. I told Ma that I'd need Tippex so as I could correct any mistakes I made. Ma was delighted.

'Our first scholar.'

Little did she know that the reason I needed so much Tippex was because I was sniffing it!

One day she came home from town laden down with bags. We were coming towards the end of the summer holidays so she'd been out shopping for school supplies. I grabbed the bags, rulers, copies, pencils, pens and fucking rubbers. 'Ma! Where's the Tippex?'

'I didn't buy any, son. It's too dear and, besides, the woman in the shop said that you're too young for Tippex and that rubbers are just as good.'

I felt like screaming. Fuck that nosy cunt in the shop . . . what does she know?!

I knew now that if I wanted Tippex, I'd have to get it myself. I headed into town and made my way to Eason's bookshop. I robbed three bottles and legged it to Lotts Lane, where I sniffed my brains out.

It didn't take long for the shops to realise why there was so much Tippex and glue going missing, so they started putting it behind the counter. This didn't bother me . . . I moved on to gas!

Gas was so much better. No more sniffing out of a bag, no

more worry about Tippex staining my clothes and Ma copping on to what I was up to. No, all I had to do with the gas was put the nozzle in between my teeth, push and hey presto! Taking gas was like taking LSD (not that I knew this at the time) but the trip didn't last as long. We used to imagine that the high we got from gas must be what it was like being in Willy Wonka's world. We were hallucinating, big time: seeing people who weren't there and the flats looking like kids' building blocks, all different shapes and colours! And the other thing about gas was that it was so easy to get. We were only thirteen but we never had a problem getting it. I used to just walk into our local shop and ask for four cans of gas for my da's lighter and they'd just give it to me. The first time I went to buy gas, I expected the man in the shop to give me a kick up the arse and send me home with an earful, but he didn't, he just handed it over. I thought I was great; I was the big man around the flats, able to get gas without a note from my da. And to think I hadn't even got hairs on my balls at the time!

It took the death of a mate, from gas, to convince me to give it up.

Snapper was sniffing gas behind the church when the guards snuck up on him. He got such a fright he just legged it . . . straight into a telegraph pole. They said that the amount of gas in his brain and the impact of the pole had done it. I lost all interest in gas after this. Some of the other lads who I bought it for tried to make me change my mind. They said the gas wouldn't cause me any problems so long as I stayed away from poles, but I wasn't convinced. Besides, I'd had enough of that chemical shite.

That's when I started on hash and ecstasy. Me and my mates would go on the rob and we'd buy hash with the proceeds. On Saturdays, we'd buy Es and head off to a rave. I always had trouble trying to get past the club bouncers. I was hanging out with older lads and they all just sailed past the bouncers and into the club, but not me, I was always stopped.

'And where do you think you're going? It's way past your bedtime!'

And then one of them would laugh like he'd just told the joke of the century . . . bastards!

But it didn't take me long to realise that everyone had their price. One night I offered one of the bouncers thirty quid to open the side door and let me in . . . I didn't have to offer twice! It was fucking daylight robbery but I didn't care. I was sick and tired listening to my mates going on about all the craic they had at the raves. There was some real shite music in the charts at the time but once I hit the dance floor it became the best music ever: 'Ebeneezer Goode' by the Shamen, and 'Rhythm is a Dancer' by Snap.

I was having the time of my life and I never wanted it to end. I was as free as the breeze . . . I didn't have a care in the world. When the rave was over, we'd head back to one of our friends' aul fella's prefabs, where we'd smoke some more hash to help us come down off the Es. I'd tell my folks that I was staying at my mate's place. There was no way I could have gone home in the state I was in. Some of the lads started taking heroin to help them come down, but I didn't. Not because I didn't want to but because I knew that Anto and Ned would fucking kill me if they heard I was taking heroin.

However, my fear of Anto and Ned didn't last long. One day I was walking down a laneway off Cork Street when I saw a fella ahead of me acting all suspicious. He was looking all around him, making sure there was no one around. I hid behind a wall and watched him; he seemed to be hiding something. I waited until he was well gone before I headed over to where he'd been. I knew the minute I saw the little bags that I had found a stash of heroin. Just because I'd never taken it, didn't mean I couldn't recognise it.

I pocketed the stash and went around to a mate who used heroin. I gave him two bags. I sat watching him as he smoked it.

'Here, give us a go.'

He freaked. 'No fucking way, David. You don't want to get mixed up in this shit.'

I kept nagging him until eventually he cracked and agreed to show me how to do it.

I vomited all over the room. I was so sick I couldn't get up off his bed. I thought I was going to die. He carried me into the spare bedroom and told me to get some sleep. There was no way he could let me go home in this state.

After that I swore I'd never touch heroin again. I couldn't understand what the big attraction was. If that was the buzz they got from heroin, they were welcome to it. I'd stick to my Es. I gave him the other four bags.

However, by the next evening I'd changed my mind. The morning after my heroin experience, I decided to go back to the laneway where I'd found it. Don't ask me why, I just did. I located the hiding place and could hardly believe my eyes when I discovered another six bags of heroin.

'Yes,' I thought. 'You fucking beaut!'

That evening I tried heroin again and this time I wasn't sick. I felt fucking brilliant! My six bags lasted for three days . . . three blissful days . . . perfection! And then it was gone.

I had to get that feeling back. I went back to the laneway, nothing. The bastard had obviously got wide. Fuck. What was I going to do? There was only one thing to do: rob.

My mates were telling me not to do it, and that I'd end up getting strung out, but I didn't listen. Anyway, what did they know? They were only jealous. Just because they were strung out, didn't mean the same thing would happen to me, it was a load of bollix. I'd been smoking gear every day for a year now and there wasn't a bother on me. I was on top of the world!

Then it happened.

I woke up one morning convinced I was dying.

I didn't know what was wrong with me; I'd never felt like this before. I must have been getting the flu.

I shouted for my mother and told her I was feeling rotten and that I didn't know what was wrong with me. I was sweating like a pig, I had a pain in my back that was shooting down my legs and I hadn't an ounce of energy.

Ma was asking me what I'd had to eat the day before. Maybe I'd eaten a curry.

''Cause you know you can get salmonella poisoning or that Newcastle's disease from dodgy chicken!'

Ma was great. She knew all about weird diseases. She took my temperature and said it was very high. She stood up.

'I'm going to call the doctor.'

Bang . . . suddenly it hit me. 'No!' I shouted.

I was so adamant about the doctor that she sussed something was up. She left the room and went across the block to a fella everyone knew was on drugs. She dragged him over to our flat and shoved him into my bedroom, the poor fella was terrified. She pointed at me and asked him what he thought was wrong with me. My eyes pleaded with him not to say anything. He tried to play dumb but Ma wasn't having any of it. And after what seemed like hours of interrogation, the poor fucker caved in. I'm convinced Ma worked for the KGB at some time in her past life.

She threw the junkie out and attacked me. When she had exhausted herself with battering me, she left the room; she was crying. What I didn't know at the time was that she went back across to the junkie and found out everything there was to know about weaning someone off drugs.

I don't know how long I slept for but when I finally woke up I felt brand new. But I still didn't get up, I knew the longer I stayed in bed, the longer it would be before I had to face Ma and Da's inquisition.

Eventually, however, I had to get up. I got dressed but I couldn't find my runners. In fact, I couldn't find any shoes! I went downstairs and asked Ma what she'd done with my runners.

'I burnt them.'

'What?'

'I burnt them!'

'Why?'

'Because if you have no runners, you can't go out. And you're not leaving this flat until I'm convinced you're clean.'

I freaked. 'Ma, I want my fucking runners!'

'I haven't got your runners. I burnt them.'

I looked at the fire. I was losing it.

'Ma, there's no fucking ashes in the poxy fire! Now where are my runners?'

She was getting annoyed, telling me not to use that language at her. I was tearing around the place, opening and closing the presses. I was frantic.

'Ma, I'll go out in my bare feet if I have to . . . I don't care.'

I left the flat wearing only socks. Ma was screaming after me to come back. I went straight to my mate's gaff and borrowed a pair of runners. It was time to start robbing again.

All that shite over my runners had annoyed me. I was fuming. The fucking cheek of her! Who did she think she was, burning my runners? Jaysus, she was treating me like a fucking prisoner in my own home!

I was furious and I knew that someone was going to get the brunt of my fury. I needed to score, so that meant that I needed money . . . fast. There was no way I was ever going to go through cold turkey again.

Me and my mate cut up an old jumper and made two balaclavas out of it. We took a hammer and a screwdriver from his da's toolbox and headed down to Cork Street to rob a car.

By the time we got to the Coombe Hospital car park, I no longer wanted to rob a car. 'Fuck the car,' I said, looking over at the shop across the road. 'Let's do that shop instead.'

'No fucking way.'

'Why not?'

'It's too close to home. Let's rob a car and head a bit further afield.'

'Fuck that, no. I'm dying sick, you're dying sick, we need money now. If you want to drive halfway around the world, be my guest. I'll do the shop on my own!'

'Do you know something, Davy? You're becoming a right moany fuck.'

I was crossing the road when he shouted after me. 'Wait up, will you?'

I looked through the shop window and saw that there were only two customers and the shopkeeper inside. My mate said that we'd make our move as soon as the customers left. But as soon as the original customers came out, others went in.

'Ah, fuck this,' I said as I ballied up and pushed through the shop door. My mate followed. Before the people in the shop knew what was happening, I was over the counter. I grabbed the shopkeeper by the scruff of the neck and, waving the hammer in the air, I shouted at him to open the cash register.

I had no intention of using the hammer. A bit of pushing

and shoving would be enough to get me what I wanted. I glanced over at my mate. He was keeping 'ello' at the door, making sure no one was coming. It was going like clockwork.

Bling!

The cash register opened and I grabbed the money (all one hundred and twenty pounds of it) and was stuffing it into my pocket. I now had the price of three bags in my pocket.

Me mate was screaming, 'Come on, the fuck.'

I was jumping over the counter when the fucking gobshite of a shopkeeper caught my leg and pulled me to the ground. I hit the floor like a brick, whacking my chin off the counter as I fell. My mate ran over and picked me up. I just lost it. I was back across the counter in a flash, swinging the hammer at the shopkeeper. I was screaming like a maniac.

'You stupid fucking cunt.'

He crumbled to the floor.

I hit him again.

Me mate was shouting at me to stop but I couldn't. I'd teach this fucker! Who did he think he was, trying to act the hero?! So he wanted to get his poxy face in the local paper? Well, I'd make sure he got his face in the fucking paper!

My mate was screaming. 'Ah, no. For fuck sake, Davy!'

'Shurrup, you! It's his own bleeding fault! He shouldn't have tried to be Charles fucking Bronson.'

'Fuck him . . . Look there!'

I looked up and saw a customer standing in the middle of the road, trying to flag down a car. I had been so preoccupied with beating the shopkeeper that I hadn't noticed the customer leaving the shop.

I screamed at my mate, 'Yeh fucking thick! You were supposed to be watching the door.'

I hit the shopkeeper one more time before jumping over the counter.

We were out of the shop and running down the street

when some fellas started to give chase. I cursed the fact that we hadn't robbed a car. A car would have made our getaway so much easier. I was feeling so sick with needing a fix that I was finding it difficult to run.

By now a few more people had joined the chase. They chased us all the way to Fatima Mansion flats before they finally gave up. They weren't stupid, they knew better than to chase us into the flats. They knew they wouldn't have got out alive!

When we got into the flats, we headed to my mate's place. The minute he closed the door, he started having a go at me, telling me what a fucking gobshite I was. And how, if he had been in charge, he wouldn't have ballsed up and landed us in all this shite!

'Ah, fuck off, you. If I listened to you, I'd never do anything. Anyway, I got the fucking money, didn't I?'

'Yeah, you got the fucking money! But what if we'd got caught? What then?'

'Well, we didn't. So shut the fuck up!'

'No fucking thanks to you!'

He was really beginning to annoy me. 'Would you ever shut fucking up! You're like a bleeding aul one. Moan-fucking-moan. Chill out, for fuck sake!'

'Why'd you have to hit the aul lad?'

''Cause he fucking pissed me off! And you're starting to piss me off too . . . just give it a fucking rest!'

I picked up the hammer and waved it at him. He jumped up.

'Gimme that fucking thing. That's fucking evidence, you thick cunt!'

We calmed down. We changed out of our filthy bloodstained clothes before heading out to score.

Once we scored our bags of heroin, we came back to the flat, cooked it up and sent it sailing through our veins.

Suddenly we were best friends again. We laughed about all that had happened that day. What had made that stupid shopkeeper fight back? I mean, all he had to do was give us the money and as soon as we'd gone call the police. Simple. Then, once he'd reported the crime to the police, he could fill out his insurance claim form and bingo! He'd have his money back in no time. But no, our little action man wanted to make a name for himself . . . another little have-a-go hero . . . just what the country needed!

Pretty soon the sickness was kicking in again and it was time to find the money for our next fix.

So now you know how it all began. Day after day, month after month, year after year. I ended up just like my brothers. All I had to look forward to was visits from my ma . . . she never did get that family portrait done.

And who did I blame? Who can I blame? No one . . . shit just happens.

Long Way from Scotland to Here – by P.J.

I have vivid memories of leaving McKerrell Street in Glasgow. Not memories about when we left, but why we left.

As far as I could understand, my aul fella had been paying too much attention to his best mate's missus and if we didn't move the aul fella was going to get seriously hurt. And there would be no fear of him fighting back, as the only people the aul fella ever raised his hand to were me and my ma. It was time we moved on. The actual moving was a neighbourly affair. The neighbours came out in their droves to say goodbye and wish us well; it was almost like a party. People from McKerrell Street thought that if you were lucky enough to be leaving that street, you must be moving up in the world. I remember one aul fella saying that McKerrell Street was so far down the ladder, the next stop was hell.

We didn't need a removal truck, as the aul fella had got the loan of a low-loader from work. It was a swan-neck trailer with two big tracks as its base and no middle, as it was normally used to transport cranes. Our furniture was tied down with rope and Ma placed tea cloths and rags on the sofa and table to protect them, even though they were so worn they were hardly worth protecting.

I asked the aul fella if it was OK for me to make a quick

49

visit around the corner to see a fella I knew. He shouted that I had five minutes to say my goodbyes. What he didn't know was that I wasn't going to say goodbye, not in the normal way anyway. I was going to beat the hell out of the fella and love every minute of it. This particular fella had always fought with me, and if I won the fight he'd get his big brother to beat the crap out of me. I wished I could have seen his face when he and his big brother came around to our street later and heard I was gone.

Looking back, I suppose we should have been embarrassed setting off with our life's possessions tied onto a low-loader, but we weren't. However, all that changed when we turned into Glasgow's Maree Road. The houses here were dead fancy and they all had a car in the driveway. The only car that had ever come to McKerrell Street was the one driven by the Provident man when he came to collect his money.

And, unlike our old neighbours, no one offered to help us move in. Instead they all stayed behind twitching curtains or stood in little packs watching us from the other side of the road. Ma, being Ma, waved a few friendly hellos but no one answered. She pulled me to her and whispered, 'If you're throwing something at those ignorant fuckers, make sure it's something that doesn't break.'

Ma was a strong person and you only got one chance with her. She only ever made one friend on Maree Road and that was the woman who moved in after us.

The aul fella left the house that night, without saying a word. And never came back. I don't know if he told Ma where he was going, she never said. When I asked her where Da was, she just said, 'You're the man of the house now.'

A week later, we received a house-warming present: someone set fire to our rubbish bin. This really annoyed Ma, as it was the first proper bin we had ever had. I was coming down the street with the shopping when I heard Ma shouting out the window to me.

'P.J., kill him.'

I looked around to see who it was I was supposed to kill but I couldn't see anyone.

'Who?'

'Him hiding over there. The little red fucker.'

I didn't know the boy from Adam but it was either fight him or face my ma. After I had beat the living daylights out of the bin-burner, Ma couldn't stop fussing over me, making me tea and giving me treats. I didn't realise that I had just taken on, and beaten, the best scrapper in the area until three nights later when a rock came through our window. Ma ran to the window and, looking out, she screamed.

'It's that little red fucker . . . the one who burnt our bin.'

I was ready to earn more brownie points. 'Don't worry ma, I'll get him.'

'Aye, see that you give him a hiding he won't forget this time, P.J.'

I assured her I would, as I headed out the door. It wasn't until I was halfway into the communal garden at the back of the house that I realised Red wasn't alone. He was with a gang of around five or six and they all got stuck in. I cried out to Ma for help. She leaned out the window.

'If you don't get up and fight like a man, you useless little fucker, you'll have me to deal with.'

When I turned eight, I got a job on a milk float. It meant I had to get up very early six days a week and work one late evening collecting the money, but the feeling I got when the milkman put my wages into my hand made it all worthwhile. And when I paid Ma her 'digs money', I felt like a million dollars. I discovered that nothing compared to the feeling you got from having your own money, and the more money I got the more I wanted. Someone told me that there was great money to be made picking potatoes during the school holidays. Ma had no objections to the fact that the spud-picking was on the other side of Scotland, seeing as how I wouldn't be alone 'cause one of my cousins was planning on doing it too. So, that was what I did for my school holiday breaks. The gaffer was always happy to see me arrive because I worked as hard as the men but he didn't have to pay me as much. Ma was happy with the extra few pounds and I always made it home for the weekends. After a while, she told me not to bother coming home every weekend, as it was a long journey and I was spending too much money on train fares. She said she had a nice nest egg saved up and if I got home once a month we'd all be much better off. So I stayed away most weekends.

At first, it was great. I stuffed my face with sweets and spent hours in the amusement arcades. That soon lost its appeal, though, so at the ripe old age of nine I found a new love . . . vodka and coke.

I was fifteen when my mother died. I was working in a spud field when I looked up and saw my uncle striding towards me. I watched him approach, thinking that perhaps he was just passing and had decided to pay me a surprise visit. My mind raced with the idea that he might get me off work early and take me to town for a treat. That hope was soon shattered, as he approached and told me brusquely, 'I've had a phone call from Ireland. Your mother's dead. Get your gear, we have to go.'

She had died while visiting her family in Donegal. I blamed myself for her death. If I hadn't given her all that money perhaps she wouldn't have died. It took a lot of convincing for me to accept that the brain haemorrhage she'd had had nothing to do with how much money she had and could have happened to anyone at any time. During the next two months in Donegal, I drank myself stupid. No one interfered or nagged me; people obviously thought it was my way of dealing with things.

Eventually it was time to go back to Scotland. My ma's sisters, Aunt Sarah and Aunt Nora, wanted to split the family up and take two kids each, the youngest going with Sarah while me and my sister were to go with Nora. I put my foot down and told them we didn't need their help, we'd be fine. We headed back to our house on Maree Road, not letting anyone know that Ma was dead, all except Ma's friend who lived next door. We knew she'd be understanding about it and help us to cope. I got my old job back on the milk float and got myself a paper round too. I continued to collect Ma's book money as I had done for years and my sister got a job in the local chipper. I stopped drinking. I just hadn't the time, what with doing two jobs, getting the kids ready for school, making dinners and doing all the housework . . . I was only beginning to realise all that Ma had done.

Eventually, however, the council got wind of our situation and we were split up and sent off to our two aunties, as they'd originally planned. I stayed at the same school, though it meant cycling an extra ten miles every day. I lost both my jobs but started making money selling loose cigarettes to snotty-nosed kids. I don't think half of them smoked but they liked to be seen buying them. I bought a twenty pack for seventy-eight pence and sold them as singles for ten pence each. Most days I sold at least two packets.

I was good at school. I hated homework, but when the teachers saw that I could pass exams without doing it they tended to leave me alone. My technical drawing teacher became something of a confidant. He had noticed my younger brother wasn't attending school, and when he asked me why, I decided to tell him. Obviously sensing that I needed an adult to talk to, he invited me to the local pub for a drink. I had got used to drinking in Donegal and so I walked up to the counter not expecting to be refused. I ordered a vodka and coke and the barman served me. The teacher couldn't believe his eyes when he saw what I was drinking. We began meeting there every Friday and I must confess that there were nights when we fell out of the place. I began to go to the pub every night after school and have a few before taking the long cycle home.

That summer I fell in with a new crowd, who lived beside my younger brother and sister. As my schooldays were well and truly over, I decided to have a break. It might be the last one I had for a long time. The new crowd loved to go ice-skating. We'd catch a train along the west coast to the Magnum Sports Centre in Irvine – a small town sixty miles or so from Glasgow. Once again I found that I adapted well, and was skating like a pro in no time. Within a few weeks I was on the ice-hockey team, even though most of the team were a few years older than me. After our Wednesday matches we'd have a few pints – nothing major, mind – and me being a shorts drinker, I'd always wrangle a few extra doubles. I'd then have a kip on the hour-and-a-half journey home and Aunt Sarah would be none the wiser. On Saturday nights we'd have a real session, and we'd all end up crashing in what one of the lads called a flat, though as far as I was concerned it was just a glorified boxroom in the West End of Glasgow. When a similar room became vacant in his building, I decided that it was time I moved out on my own too.

Once I moved into my new home, my first task was to visit every pub in the vicinity. I was halfway through the challenge, and very unimpressed with them all, when I stumbled upon The Pyramid. The first thing I noticed upon entering were the two blondes serving behind the bar. I was glad to see that they seemed to notice me too. It wasn't until we got talking that I realised I was the first customer to grace this new bar. The girls' chatty demeanour encouraged me to stay put for the rest of the night. I even earned myself a free pint by helping them to throw out their first dodgy drunken customer . . . things were looking up.

One of the girls had just moved into a flat across the road and hadn't made any friends since coming to Glasgow from the Highlands. I managed to wangle an invite to her place for a 'nightcap'. Being from the back of beyond, she lapped up my urban stories and I got a great kick from her continually commenting that I was mad. That night we started a very intimate relationship that was to last for a number of months. It was the perfect romance. I spent my evenings and the early part of the night in the bar and when she was finished work we'd go back to her place and have a few cans or a bottle of vodka and a bit of what comes naturally.

As with anyone, money for me was tight every now and again, but I always needed a drink and I had to find the extra cash to get it. I'd managed to blag my way into a cushy number in a small accounts office, and within a few weeks I knew the run of the place. One evening, before I left work, I checked the petty cash box. I was very happy to see there was over nine hundred quid in it. It was almost embarrassing how easy it was to rob. The next day no one mentioned the petty cash box, the only comment to me was that I looked a bit under the weather or maybe I was burning the candle at both ends . . . I wasn't even in the running for suspicion of thieving.

I kept to my routine of drinking every night until I was skint and then I'd rob the petty cash box again. Robbing the petty cash was becoming a bit of a ritual. I decided that the best way to stay free from suspicion was to make sure that, on the days following a robbery, I showed up for work looking like I'd had a good night's sleep and not like someone who'd been out on the tiles all night . . . but as they say . . . the best-laid plans nearly always go astray!

After a few weeks of robbing the cash box, I began to throw caution to the wind. I stayed at Blondie's flat drinking till the early hours of the morning and only left when I knew the off-licence would be open. One morning I went to buy a bottle of vodka from the local corner shop but as I tried to leave the shop I found that the door was jammed. The old Pakistani man who owned the shop came to my assistance and showed me how to open the door, explaining that it was an old latch and was always acting up. As I watched him fiddling with the dodgy latch, I noticed that this was the only lock on the door. I stored this information and headed home. On the way I stopped off to buy some square sliced sausage, the staple diet of the lower classes, which I would devour before I headed back to The Pyramid later that evening. As I stood in the butcher's, my eyes were drawn to the biggest knife I had ever seen. While the butcher was in the freezer getting my meat, I acted on impulse and grabbed the knife and stuffed it into my bag.

I was drinking more and more. Money was slipping through my fingers like water. One night when I went to get the petty cash box, I noticed that it only had about three hundred quid in it, but I decided to rob it anyway. This time, however, I was going to raid the boss's drinks cabinet too. His Scotch would do nicely for what had become a very expensive home-drinking habit. As usual, everything went like clockwork. I even had time to do some very artistic graffiti. I was on my way out the door, when I sensed someone behind me.

'Will that alarm go off in a few minutes?'

I knew without looking that it was a copper, a young copper. Without thinking, I turned and hit him with the bottle of Scotch. I ran through all the side streets until I reached The Pyramid, where I sat drinking for the rest of the night. I knew that things had changed forever. I couldn't go back to work because the copper would easily recognise me, and I knew that once I failed to show up for work the boss would put two and two together and finger me. I was finished.

For five days, I drank non-stop. I thought about my sisters and my brother, about work, about the policeman. I couldn't sleep; I just lay on the bed in a subhuman state. Eventually, I'd had enough. I had to give myself up. If I got sent to prison for a while it might do me good, might help me to break the stronghold that the drink was beginning to have on me. I was barely seventeen and was already on the road to alcoholism.

I walked into the police station and straight up to the overweight sergeant dozing behind the desk and blurted out, 'I've been robbing the office where I work. I need to talk to someone about it.'

That woke the lazy bastard up. He looked me up and down. It was obvious from my clothes that I wasn't a down and out. He looked me straight in the eyes, obviously trying to decide if I was winding him up. Eventually, he must have believed me because he pointed to the reception room and told me to sit in there and wait.

Time passed slowly. I was starting to visualise all kinds of terrible things. They'd give me life for hitting a police officer. I imagined myself ending up like the Count of Monte Cristo. A detective came into the reception room and told me to follow him. I thought 'this is it', but he calmly led me to a desk in a packed office, told me to take a seat and then asked me if I'd like tea or coffee.

I told him everything. How many times I'd robbed the offices, how much money I'd got, the system I'd used. He never said a word. He just sat there staring at me, looking totally dumbfounded. The only part of the story I left out was the bit where I'd hit the copper with the whisky bottle. I figured they'd work that out for themselves and when they did I wouldn't deny it. I'd just say I didn't remember, it must have happened when I had drink on. When I finished my story, I expected him to freak out, but he didn't, he just sat back in his chair and asked me why?

'Drink,' I replied.

The detective picked up his phone and phoned the thick little Belfast bastard who was my boss. The boss more or less agreed with what I had told the detective: dates on which money had been stolen, amounts, etc. The detective put down the phone and smiled at me.

'You're sacked.'

The whole interview lasted no more than a couple of hours.

'OK, you can go now. We'll send you notice of your court date through the post.'

'So you're not locking me up?'

'No. Seeing as you gave yourself up, you can go home.'

He must have seen the shocked look on my face.

'What's the matter, son?' he asked.

'I only gave myself up 'cause I was sure you'd lock me up.'

'Why would you want to be locked up?'

'To get off the drink, I know I can't do it by myself.'

'Sorry, son, it doesn't work like that.'

I left the police station feeling disgusted with the whole charade. It had been a complete waste of time.

When I got home, I took my big knife that I'd stolen from the butcher's and went out and robbed the Pakistani shop. I had never felt anything like the adrenalin rush I got when I got home with a bag of smokes and cash. Drink had never made me feel like this. I began robbing a shop a week. It was a piece of cake. Most of the shops only had a hall-door latch and none of them had security cameras. I'd stand across the road watching the shops and wait until there were no customers inside. Then I'd walk across to the shop, open the door and close the latch behind me. I'd ask the shopkeeper for cigarettes, which were always on a shelf behind him, and as soon as he turned his back I'd follow him behind the counter and take out the knife. Once they saw the knife, they didn't say a word, just filled my bag with cigarettes and money.

Only once it didn't work; the old Pakistani wouldn't open the till. I wasn't going to stab someone for a few bob so I legged it, getting a smack of a flying hammer for my troubles. Normally the whole operation would take less than three minutes.

My barmaid girlfriend loved hearing about my escapades. The Pyramid now had quite a few regulars who loved swapping war stories. My girlfriend was always egging me on to tell them my stories. So I did. I told them all about the petty cash box, about how I'd handed myself in to the police and about how easy it was to rob a corner shop. I could tell by the looks on their faces that they thought I suffered from an overactive imagination. I knew they were thinking I only made up the stories to impress my barmaid girlfriend, who loved the idea of going out with a Robin Hood-type character.

To prove that I was telling the truth, I decided to put on an exhibition. The Pyramid was on the Great Western Road in the west end of Glasgow, which was one of the widest roads in the west end. Almost directly across the road from the pub was a Pakistani shop. They could watch me doing a robbery from the comfort of the pub. I walked out across to the shop as cool as if I was going to buy a pint of milk. I even waved before I entered the shop.

Three minutes later I was back in my seat at the bar with all the regulars sitting looking at me in disbelief. I bought a round of drinks and for the rest of the night I sat back and enjoyed being the centre of attention.

One day the owner of The Pyramid pulled me to one side and told me that he knew what I was up to. I was sure he was going to bar me, but instead he gave me an earful about doing Mickey Mouse jobs. As far as he was concerned, someone with my bottle should be doing decent jobs and making enough money to live off them for months. And surprise, surprise, it just so happened that he knew of the ideal job for me. It turned out that before he'd bought The Pyramid he'd worked for some old fucker whom he'd hated. The old man thought he was a bit of a gangster and liked to pay all his bills with cash. Because of this, he always had a lot of cash lying around. The publican was so confident that this job was worth doing that he told me if I got anything less than ten grand I could keep it for myself . . . all he wanted was revenge on the old bastard and my word that this job was just between him and me.

Three nights later I got a taxi to the aul man's pub. I ate a bag of chips while I waited for the aul lad to lock up and leave for the night. The funny thing was that I was more scared in an empty pub than I ever was robbing a shop. I fumbled around in the dark until I found my way to the basement, and after a bit of rummaging around I found what I was looking for . . . a crate full of money!

On my way out I nabbed a bottle of whisky. So, with my bag of money and my celebratory bottle, I headed back to my flat. I didn't even bother counting the money, I simply got myself drunk.

The next afternoon I went into The Pyramid and took great pleasure in winding the owner up about how much I'd got from the aul lad's pub. He told me he didn't care about the money.

'Sure, you'll end up putting most of it in my till anyway.'

He was right. Apart from sending a few bob to my family and getting some nice clothes, the vast majority of the money found its way into The Pyramid's till. The only person I told about the job was my barmaid girlfriend. I couldn't help myself. She always got turned on by my escapades and fucked like the proverbial rabbit. The only part of the story that I didn't tell her was the part that concerned her boss.

Out of the blue a copper appeared at my door and handed me a summons to appear in court. Having never received a summons before, I didn't know what I was supposed to do with it. I went down to the police station and asked the detective I'd spoken to before what exactly it meant. He gave me the name of a lady solicitor and told me to go and see her, as she was really good and totally straight. The solicitor told me that if it was just the theft of the petty cash box, I would get less than a year but with the assault on the police officer I would probably get four. I assured her that the copper wouldn't recognise me, as he hadn't got a good look at my face. She looked me straight in the eyes and sighed.

'You really are very naive, aren't you? The policeman who handed you your summons was the policeman you assaulted. Now who do you think a judge is going to believe? An upstanding enforcer of the law or a self-confessed robber?'

What a downer. I was determined to enjoy the next few weeks, for they might have been my last days of freedom. However, no matter how hard I tried, I couldn't stop thinking about jail. I wanted to enjoy my new-found wealth but I knew that my days were numbered.

I was on my way down to the Court House when, like a sign from God, it appeared before me . . . McGinley's Donegal Coach. The driver told me I had an hour before he would be leaving. I took a taxi to my flat and packed as many of my new clothes as possible into a case.

With my new clobber and dwindling fortune, I headed for Ireland.

Ever since I could remember, whenever we travelled on a bus from Glasgow to Donegal, we always got out at Quinn's Pub. We then basically waited there until someone agreed to give us a lift the seven miles to the back of the hill where our relations lived.

This time, however, I was alone. Jimmy Quinn, who ran the pub, knew my family well. Jimmy was surprised to see me, as normally word of our travels would have reached the small town weeks before us. I told Jimmy some story about me having a month off work so as I could decide what direction my life was going to take. He moaned that it was unfair that I should have a month off when he hadn't had a break in the last seven years.

As it was a quiet night in the pub, we decided that I would work the night with him in return for his hospitality. During this shift, I stupidly agreed to look after the pub for a while so he could get away for a well-earned break.

Over the next week, he showed me the ropes. I would help out here and there with customers, lighting fires and cleaning up. Then, as soon as the last customer left (they were never thrown out), Jimmy and I would sit till all hours chatting and supping. Even though the pub never seemed busy, I assumed he was doing well, and it wasn't until he was gone that I realised what dire straits the pub was in. All the stock he possessed was on display. On my first night running the pub two good things happened: the first being the fact that there was hardly any customers; the second that my uncle came in. He was shocked to see me but I quickly told him the same story I had told Jimmy, and he seemed satisfied. He also had a solution to my lack of stock. He drove a few miles out the road to a pub he knew well and persuaded them to give me a loan of supplies until Jimmy got back. When I saw the amount of stock he brought back, I told him I'd never sell that in two weeks in Quinn's. My uncle just smiled and told me not to hold my breath waiting for Jimmy to come back. After all, Jimmy's father had popped out for a pint of milk seven years ago and hadn't been seen since.

As it happened, Jimmy did stay away for a bit longer than the two weeks originally agreed . . . he stayed away for a year and a half! After a few weeks, I resigned myself to the fact that I was stuck here until Jimmy came back. Out of complete boredom, I decided to try my hand at a bit of decorating. Nothing radical, just a lick of paint and a new carpet. I'd found a roll of carpet upstairs. That lazy bastard Jimmy had bought it but hadn't bothered to lay it. I didn't realise what a difference I'd made to the pub until I saw the stunned looks on the faces of the customers. Some of the punters (those in their thirties) had been too young to drink the last time Quinn's had been decorated. News soon travelled of the newly refurbished Quinn's and I had a busy festive season because of it. I seemed to get along well with my new customers and they soon made Quinn's their local. With my weekends more or less sorted, I decided to concentrate on putting bums on seats midweek. We had a pool table but no pool team, and a dartboard with no darts team. Within the month, I had two teams sorted.

After six months at the helm, I hit my first major problem. Quinn's was beginning to do very well: weekends were busy and midweek our darts and pool teams kept the till looking healthy. I was taking in a lot of money but I didn't know where to put it. I didn't want to lodge these new amounts into Jimmy's bank account, as I was sure he would get a call from the taxman. I decided that I would stash the extra cash anywhere I could and let Jimmy sort it out when he got back.

During my whole time running the pub, there were two

things that struck me as funny. The first was that, from start to finish, I hardly drank a drop. The second was that, even though no one would have known how much money the pub was making, I never took a penny.

By the time Jimmy did return, the pub was a little gold mine. I had the darts on a Monday and Wednesday and pool on Tuesday and Thursday. On Friday I had two fellas from Letterkenny who played the flute and the fiddle. The weekends looked after themselves. I even had to employ a couple of local women to help me out now and then.

When Jimmy finally arrived back, he acted very strange. He stayed upstairs all day and only came down to the bar whenever the last customer had left and I had gone to bed. I sometimes sat at the bar alone having a pint, just to see if he would come down for a chat, like the old times, but he never opened his bedroom door until I'd closed mine. We had barely said two words to each other during the first week he was home. One night, hearing him go downstairs, I followed him. The minute he saw me, he came at me with an accusing attitude, wanting to know where I'd got the money to redecorate the pub. I had a smile on my face as I told him that doing the pub up had cost nothing and I had loads of money tucked away waiting for his return. I went to my hideouts and pulled out wads of cash and brought it down to him. When I placed a pile in front of him, I told him there was lots more but I couldn't remember where I'd hidden it. It was the first time I'd heard him laugh since he'd come back. He took the money up to his room, came back and got me pissed. However, the next morning he reverted back to the old Jimmy, sleeping by day and drinking by night.

Nothing much changed over the next few months. I was happy enough looking after Quinn's. I had my own room, food, drink, cigarettes, and I even had a night out when the darts or pool teams played away. Life was good.

One day, all this changed. I went out for a breath of fresh air and when I came back my bags were on the doorstep. I didn't have a key so I climbed in a small window at the back of the pub. Jimmy was sitting at the bar, pissed. He was ranting and raving about my living under his roof rent-free. He told me it was time I left and stood on my own two feet. I could have argued with him. I could have told him that in my two years of working day and night I had never taken a penny, but what would be the point? I walked outside, picked up my bags and stuck out my thumb, not knowing where I was going.

The first car that came along stopped.

'Where are you going?' I asked the driver.

'Dublin,' he replied.

'Well, Dublin it is then.'

Little did I know what Dublin would have in store for me. I'd meet, fall in love with and eventually marry one of the first girls I saw. I'd also come across an opportunity that was too good to miss, an opportunity to make a small fortune, an opportunity which would end up landing me in prison, but that, as they say, is another story.

Easy Money – by A.D.

The buzzing of the alarm clock announced the time as 9 a.m., but Tommy didn't need an alarm clock, he was already awake. Tommy had been awake since 7 a.m., but not because he was an early bird and anxious to greet the new day, oh no. The reason Tommy was awake so early was that his head was throbbing, due to the amount of drink he'd had the night before. He really needed some headache tablets, but hadn't the energy to climb out of bed to get them.

Instead he just lay there trying to remember the night before. Another Monday night wasted, he thought. How come he always ended up spending nearly every penny of his dole money in one single night?

He reached for a cigarette, muttering to himself. 'Jaysus, Tommy, you're an awful bollox . . . will you never learn?'

It was hard to believe that a couple of months ago he had been living the high life in London. But the high life had gone up in smoke the day his wife announced that she was leaving him for her boss. Tommy couldn't believe it.

'But you said you didn't even like the fucker! A smarmy little shit in a fake Armani suit is what you called him!'

'Yeah, well, I've changed my mind about him.'

Although he knew that things hadn't been good between them for a long time, he'd never thought for one minute that they'd split up or that she'd have an affair! However, the memory of Mr Armani on his knees, crying, as his five bed-roomed house and his BMW convertible burnt to the ground brought a smile to Tommy's face.

Tommy had arrived home to Cork with ten quid in his pocket and a small hold-all carrying all his possessions, not much to show for someone who was supposed to be living the high life. But he was slowly getting his life back on track. His dole money never went very far but at least he had his own flat – a small two-roomed affair on the north side of Cork – and his friends made sure he never went without.

He reached out and turned off the radio alarm. The music was doing his head in – boom, boom, boom. He really needed to sort out his hangover. He reached for his trousers and searched his pockets. He was looking for a joint . . . he didn't find one.

'Fuck it, I could have sworn I had half a joint somewhere.'

He searched the ashtray and found his half-joint buried amongst the stubbed-out cigarette butts. Lighting the joint, he lay back and sighed.

'C'mon, Tommy, there has to be more to life than this.'

He got up, dressed, filled the sink with cold water and submerged his head in it until he couldn't hold his breath any longer. Having done this three times, he started to feel better. He grabbed his jacket and headed out the door.

As he made his way to the pub, the cold morning air caught at his smoke-filled lungs, causing him to cough uncontrollably.

'Jaysus, that's the worst thing about all this good clean Cork air . . . it fucks you up good and proper!'

As he walked down Fairhill, the traffic was light and the birds sang merrily as they sat perched on the rooftops and the church spires. He imagined they were singing 'The Boys of Fairhill'. He smiled to himself and hummed along with them.

Five hundred yards down the hill he reached his destination – The Wolfe Tone Bar. The Wolfe Tone Bar was a small dirty public house that stank of stale beer, smoke and Jeyes Fluid. The only clientele were old men and criminals who knew each other's business and didn't welcome newcomers. A lot of wheeling and dealing went on in the darkened corners of the pub, and if you were a newcomer or a nosy fucker you could easily end up a bloodied mess in the back lane with no one having seen or heard a thing.

As Tommy reached the pub door, he bumped into a man who was on his way out.

'Sorry, mate, I didn't see you there. I'm gaspin' for a curer.'

'No prob . . .' The man's voice trailed off. 'Tommy! Jaysus, boy, how the fuck are you? I heard you were back.'

Tommy stood at the open door. 'Well, Donie, seeing as you're so happy to see me, you can buy me a drink.'

Donie laughed. 'Jaysus, boy, some things never change. You're like a pair of knickers . . . always on the bum.'

When they entered the pub, Donie pointed to a darkened corner and told Tommy to go and sit down while he got the drinks in. Tommy smiled as he sat down. Donie was a great man for darkened corners. He might be only telling you what he had for his breakfast, but he insisted on doing so in a darkened corner where no one would overhear. Donie joined Tommy at the table with two pints of Heineken and two Southern Comforts. Toasting each other's health, they knocked back the chasers.

Donie shook his head. 'I can't believe you've been home for six months and I haven't set eyes on you. So, c'mon, fill me in on what's been happening.'

Over the next couple of hours, Tommy brought Donie up to date on the last eight years of his life. Donie was a great man for listening, and he never interrupted, with the result that you ended up telling him things you'd never tell anyone else . . . all your closely guarded secrets would just come tumbling out.

Seamus, the barman, kept the drinks flowing, on the house. He was an old mate of the two men and wouldn't allow them to pay for anything as long as he was behind the bar.

'Will it be OK if I join you when my shift finishes?'

'We'd be angry if you didn't.'

When Seamus joined the lads, the conversation opened up. They talked about Cork City's chances in the league, they argued whether Roy Keane, Denis Irwin or Sonia O'Sullivan was the greatest sportsperson to come out of Cork. When they had exhausted all sports conversation, Tommy asked, 'And what about you two? What have ye been up to?'

'Ah, yer know yerself . . . a bit of this . . . a bit of that.'

'It's the bit of "that" that I'm interested in, boys,' said Tommy. They all laughed, but Tommy continued. 'I'm serious, lads. I'm skint. I need a job . . . something that will give me easy money . . . and quick.'

Seamus and Donie glanced at each other, then, huddling a bit closer, Donie said, 'Well, now that you mention it, we have something in mind.'

'What?'

Donie tapped his nose. 'All in good time. You know me, Tommy, I play my cards close to my chest.'

'Well, whatever it is . . . you can count me in.'

Seamus laughed. 'We already have.'

Tommy looked puzzled. Donie laughed. 'You really think I bumped into a big fucker like you by accident?'

Two nights later, the three men sat outside of the farmers' co-op.

'What the fuck are we doing here?' Tommy asked.

The other two said nothing.

'You're not trying to tell me we're going to rob the co-op?'

'Exactly.'

'For fuck sake, Donie, there's no money in farming. Do you not listen to the farmers? They're lucky if they get a hundred quid for a cow these days.'

'Shows what you know. I was talking to an aul fella in the pub last March and he was telling me that he wanted to buy some new farming machinery. And do you know where he got the money from?' He pointed towards the co-op. 'One hundred thousand they gave him . . . cash.'

'Cash!'

'That's what I said, boy.'

Tommy let out a low whistle. 'Jaysus, what kind of farm machinery costs that kind of money?'

'Well, it obviously wasn't a wheelbarrow!' Donie laughed.

Seamus wasn't amused. 'It doesn't matter what kind of machinery he bought, the point is they were able to give him the CASH to buy it.'

Tommy turned to Seamus. 'Jaysus, lighten up, Sea . . .'

'Don't tell me to lighten up. We're not here to discuss the price of farm machinery.'

'I'm only sayi . . .'

'Well, don't only say! We're here to plan a job.'

Donie tried to calm things down. 'Will you two give it a rest? You're going to bring attention on us if ye carry on like that. Anyway, Tommy, that's only the tip of the iceberg. There's going to be a farm machinery sale next week and I have it on good authority that there'll be half a million quid sitting in that building.'

'And what about security?'

'There won't be any. It seems the co-op doesn't like to bring too much attention to the place, so they tend to run things just like any normal day.'

Tommy sat looking at the co-op. Seamus turned to him.
'You seem nervous.'

'Naw, I'm not nervous, just thinking.'

Donie started the car. 'So, Tommy, can I take it you're in?'

Tommy smiled. 'What do you think?'

Seamus and Donie planned things well, on a strictly need-to-know basis. Seamus told Tommy to expect a phone call.

'When?'

'When we're ready.'

Eventually the call came.

'Where are ye?'

'Look out your window.'

Tommy looked out and saw Donie's car parked across the road.

'Get your skates on.'

When Tommy came down, the two boys were singing along to Billy Joel's 'Piano Man'.

He laughed. The DJ's voice came over the radio. 'And that was Billy Joel's "Piano Man", taken from . . .'

'Jesus,' shouted Seamus, slapping the dashboard. 'I hate that!'

'Hate what?' Tommy asked.

'Fucking DJs butting in like that when the song's not even finished.'

Donie winked at Tommy.

'And do you know what, Se? If it was a Boyzone song, he'd play the whole fucking thing.'

Seamus took the bait. 'Don't I know it, Donie? Don't I fucking know it?!'

Tommy decided to get in on this wind-up.

'I hear your man Ronan Keating's done a cover version of "Piano Man" . . .'

'Ah, no. Not that fucking dipstick!'

'Yeah, I heard it on the radio this morning.'

'Do you know what, Tommy? There should be a law against that cunt doing covers.'

'Ah, he's OK.'

'OK?! Are you fucking mad?' He turned to face Tommy. 'There's no fan of Ronan-fucking-Keating coming on this job.'

Tommy laughed and Seamus realised it was all a wind-up. 'You little fucker, Tommy, you had me going there.'

Donie started the car. Tommy would have liked to know where they where heading but decided against asking. Sometimes, just before a job was about to happen, lads got paranoid, so it was better not to ask too many questions. Seamus was in great form, singing along to the radio and filling them full of useless information about the singers, songs, etc. They heard all about the birth of Motown Records, about how shite U2 had been when they played Slane. He brought them up to date on every concert that was going to happen in Cork that year.

Just before they reached Limerick, Seamus indicated that Donie should take a right turn that led into an old petrol station. The place looked run-down and derelict. It was like one of those isolated gas stations you'd see in an American movie. Donie parked the car at the back of the petrol station. Seamus got out. The others watched him as he made his way over to an old school bus.

He opened up the side panel and took out a toolbag, then made his way back to the car. As soon as Seamus had put the toolbag into the boot, Donie started the engine.

No sooner were they back on the road than Seamus produced a scanner from under his seat. He tuned it to the *garda* frequency to find out where all the *garda* speed checks were, so they could avoid them as they drove back to Cork. Tommy figured that the bag Seamus had taken from the bus contained guns, otherwise why would he be so worried about being stopped by the guards?

When they arrived back at Tommy's flat, Seamus got out of the van and handed him the hold-all.

'There's oil in the bag too. Make sure you clean them up.'

'Seamus, I'm not happy about this.'

Seamus smiled, but Tommy could see the evil in his eyes.

'And what did you think tonight was about? Did you think I had fuck all to do so I decided to take you out for a drive?'

'No, but . . .'

'But nothing! In this game you can trust no one. I know you're a sound bloke but I wouldn't trust my own granny on this job. So I protect myself; I make sure everyone gets their hands dirty. That way, there'll be no slip-ups . . . get my drift, kid?'

Tommy nodded then said, 'Just one more thing, Seamus.'

'What's that, kid?'

'Stop calling me kid!'

They laughed, and as Tommy opened the car door Seamus smiled. 'You're OK, kid. You're OK.'

The week passed by, slowly and uneventfully.

Tommy checked out the guns; they were good quality. Two nice sawn-off pump-action shotguns cut to two and a quarter feet . . . classic! And enough ammo to take out a small army, plus a .9 mm Beretta handgun. Tommy had to confess that this was a well-thought-out job.

Tommy stood in front of the full-length mirror that was stuck on the outside of the wardrobe door. He felt like Robert De Niro's character from *Taxi Driver*, Travis Bickle. He pulled one gun, then two, then all three at his reflection.

'You looking at me?'

He loaded the gun and cocked it at the mirror. He snarled, then smiled, at his reflection. He continued to pose in front of the mirror until he got bored, then he went back to watching television.

The night before the robbery was endless. He tried to sleep but couldn't. He twisted and turned, checked the guns over and over again until finally he fell asleep as the milk float passed his window. The persistent ringing of the doorbell woke him. He jumped up; someone was throwing pebbles at the window. He pulled back the curtains. Donie was standing on the road, looking up. When he saw Tommy, he pointed to his watch.

'Eight bells. C'mon the fuck.'

Tommy opened the window and leaned out.

'You're early, give me five minutes.'

Donie went back to the car. Seamus was sitting in the driver's seat tapping the steering wheel.

Tommy closed the window and went to turn off the alarm that had just started to buzz. There were three things Tommy hated about mornings: too much noise, being rushed and chatty, happy morning people. Tommy needed time to gather his thoughts. This was looking like a bad day.

He brushed his teeth, smoked half a joint and doused his face with cold water. Then he grabbed the hold-all and left the flat. As he reached the car, Seamus started beeping the horn.

'Ah, fuck off!' thought Tommy as he got in.

Donie pointed to the hold-all and asked, 'So, what do you think, are they good?'

'Fucking perfect. I'd like to test them first, though.'

'No time, kid.'

'Well, hopefully we won't need to use them.'

Seamus drove off, taking his time and making sure all rules of the road were adhered to. He didn't want to risk drawing any unnecessary attention to them all. As they drove along, Donie ran over the final details.

'You and Seamus will have the sawn-offs. I'll take the Beretta, as I'll be the one grabbing the cash. You two cover the floor, OK?'

The lads hesitated; Donie got nervous.

'I said, OK?'

They both nodded. He continued. 'I mean it, lads, I don't want any fuck-ups. If anyone gives you hassle or tries to be a hero, I want you to smash their fucking skulls in with the butt of your gun . . . understood?'

Tommy looked at him. 'OK. Relax, Donie, we know what we have to do. But, like I said, hopefully it won't come to that.'

They drove to a derelict factory on the outskirts of Mallow and pulled in beside a Hiace van. Without a word, they climbed into the Hiace and, slamming the door behind him, Seamus opened a new hold-all and handed out overalls and balaclavas. With his overalls on and his bally turned into a monkey cap, Seamus pulled out an old pair of runners from under the front seat.

'Ah, fuck,' said Tommy, looking at the runners. 'I forgot to bring mine. I had them out and all.'

'Well, it's too late to do anything about it now. You'll just have to wear your shoes.'

Tommy was pissed off. He knew Seamus was right but he was wearing his good shoes and he didn't want to have to burn them. Still, if the job went off as well as Donie predicted, he'd have enough money to buy hundreds of fucking shoes!

Seamus drove the Hiace onto the road. He turned on the radio and Springsteen was singing 'Born to Run'. There was something about the song that got them all pumped up. Seamus was shitting on about how Springsteen was nothing without the E Street Band. Tommy didn't give a fuck about Springsteen or his band, all he wanted to do was get the job done. Right now, he felt like he was going to throw up. He tried taking deep breaths.

Seamus told them they were almost there. Donie cocked

Seamus's sawn-off and placed it on the front seat beside him. Tommy held onto the handle on the side door and had it primed to go the minute the van stopped.

Before the handbrake was in place, Seamus was out and running. Tommy bolted from the Hiace and ran alongside Seamus. Donie was two yards behind. The main doors to the co-op were open and there were pallets of cow feed and fertiliser stacked to the roof on either side of them. The office was a Portakabin at the end of the factory.

Three casual workers were sitting on a forklift, chatting and drinking tea. The biggest of them did a double-take as the trio came running in. The big man was about to get up and confront them when Seamus kicked him square in the face. The sound of smashing teeth and bone seemed to ring through the whole building.

Tommy and Donie kept running. Tommy reached the Portakabin first. Behind him, he could hear Seamus.

'On the fucking ground . . . now!'

The commotion had obviously been heard in the Portakabin. As Tommy went to kick the door in, it opened and his boot connected with a small woman, sending her flying across the room. Tommy pointed his gun at two suits that were standing like rabbits caught in the headlights.

'Don't even think about moving.'

Donie ran to the safe and, waving his Beretta, shouted at the woman.

'Open the fucking thing.'

She was crying, holding her face. Her mouth was bleeding. He grabbed her by the hair.

'Are you fucking deaf? I said, open it!'

One of the suits went to move, but Tommy pushed his shotgun into the man's chest.

'Don't get fucking brave, mister!'

The suit held up a key. 'This is what you're looking for.'

Donie grabbed the key and went to the safe. The man looked at him. 'You're making a big mistake, boys.'

Donie opened the safe and smiled at the sight before him. It was a large safe and was stuffed full of cash.

'Walk away, boys, walk away now and we'll pretend like nothing has happened.'

Donie shouted at Tommy as he opened up a black refuse sack. 'Shut that fucker up.'

Tommy plunged the gun into the man's chest. 'Right, over there, beside her. On the ground.'

The younger of the two men did as he was told, but the older man hesitated. Tommy poked the gun hard into his stomach. 'Now.'

The man stumbled to his knees but kept his eyes on Tommy. Tommy had never seen such piercing eyes before in his life. This guy wasn't afraid. Tommy could never understand why people got in the way of an armed robbery. For God's sake, what was the point? Sure, weren't these places insured to the hilt? And besides, what chance did he have against a bullet? It was fucking stupid, but every once in a while you came up against some have-a-go hero wanting to make a name for himself.

Donie emptied the safe and struggled to the Hiace with the loaded refuse sack. When he'd put the bag into the Hiace, he shouted for the others to follow him. Tommy pulled all the phones out of their sockets.

'Don't even think about moving for another ten minutes.'

The older man looked Tommy straight in the eyes. 'You've just signed your own death warrant. You hear that, boy?'

A shiver ran down Tommy's back. 'Shut the fuck up.'

He backed out the door and made his way towards Seamus. Seamus was pointing his gun at the three casual workers; they didn't move a muscle. Seamus started moving towards the Hiace.

'Keep an eye on these three until I get her started.' He pointed to the big man. 'And if he so much as moves, stick a bullet in him.'

Minutes later, they were driving at speed back to the derelict factory and their car. Seamus was whooping like a rodeo cowboy.

'Yeeeeha! We did it, boys.'

They all laughed.

Tommy turned to Donie. 'Jesus Christ, Donie. How much was in there?'

'A few hundred grand.'

Seamus rolled down his window and howled like a wolf. Tommy looked at Donie and started doing the same.

They collected their car from the derelict factory and, as they drove away with the smell of petrol in their nostrils, the billowing black smoke was all that was left of the Hiace, overalls, balaclavas and shoes.

Seamus was once again driving at normal speed. 'Where to now, boys?'

Tommy suggested his place. 'No one knows where I live.'

Donie and Seamus agreed.

'Besides,' added Tommy, 'I need to get a pair of shoes. I look like a fucking gobshite in my bare feet!'

The others laughed. 'And I could do with a change of underpants.'

Seamus slapped the steering wheel. 'You'll need to change more than your underpants, boyo . . . cause we're gonna party tonight!'

Donie snapped at him. 'No, we're not!'

'What do you mean, no?'

'Are you totally fucking stupid? Why don't we just put a notice on our heads? "We've just robbed the co-op."'

Seamus looked sheepish. 'Sorry, Donie, I wasn't thinking.'

Donie smiled. 'Well, it's lucky one of us is. Doesn't mean we can't have a few bevies, though.'

Tommy was relieved that the tension had lifted. 'Why don't you drop me and Donie off at my gaff while you go and ditch the car? We can order a takeaway while we count the dosh.'

Seamus nodded. 'Sounds good to me.'

When Seamus arrived at Tommy's flat, he had a case of Heineken under his arm and an ounce of coke in his pocket.

'So, what have you two been up to while I was away?'

Donie smiled. 'Counting.'

Tommy added, 'I swear, I'll be seeing hundred-euro notes in my fucking sleep.'

'So how much do we have?'

'Eight hundred and twenty-nine grand and still counting . . .'

'Fuck me.'

Donie snorted a line of coke. 'What I suggest is this: after we've sorted out the expenses, we take two hundred and fifty grand each and throw the rest to Seamus's contact in the co-op. What do you say?'

'I say, yeah. He'll be more than happy with that.'

They partied hard in the flat that night. They all agreed that no one would spend big for a few months; they'd wait until the heat had died down.

The next morning, Tommy got up and told the lads he was going for a shower, as he had to head out.

'Today is dole day.'

The others laughed.

'Well, I'm entitled to it, aren't I?'

Tears were running down Donie's face.

'What are you laughing at? You told us to act normal, didn't you?'

'Yeah, I know, and you're right. It's just the thought of you queuing for half the fucking day to collect a few scabby euros when you have all this money here.'

Tommy was surprised that no one was talking about the co-op robbery in the post office. He bought a few newspapers but there was nothing in them. When he got back to the flat, he turned on the radio but there was nothing on that either.

'Maybe,' Donie offered, 'they're keeping it quiet, hoping someone will slip up.'

'More likely they're embarrassed about having all that money and no security,' said Seamus.

'True,' agreed Tommy. 'If the lads get wind of how easy it is to rob that place, there'll be a queue down the street waiting to do it.'

Around mid-morning, they split up, having agreed to meet up for a pint in The Wolfe Tone later on that day. Each man wanted time to himself, and a little privacy when it came to hiding his stash.

They must have had a good time in The Wolfe Tone, because the next morning Tommy couldn't even remember how he got home. He lit a joint and then snorted the last of the coke before checking his stash. Everything was OK.

He was happy he still had the guns under his bed too. It was nice to know he had protection, just in case someone came sniffing around.

Slowly, Tommy began spending his money from the co-op robbery. Nothing extravagant, mind. Just a couple of pairs of jeans, a nice jacket, shoes and a television with matching DVD. He stocked up his fridge and, for the first time since coming back to Cork, he ate well on a daily basis.

It was strange that no one was talking about the co-op. The Wolfe Tone usually buzzed with news of the latest robberies. If so much as a pint of milk was stolen on the main street, you'd hear about it in The Wolfe Tone. So the fact that no one was talking about the co-op was very strange indeed.

On the other side of the river, Donie was being equally careful. No big purchases, just a steady stream of small items, nothing that would bring attention to him. A pity the same couldn't be said about Seamus. He left his job as a barman and began frequenting the lap-dancing clubs that were beginning to spring up around town. Seamus was beginning to look like a cheap pimp, with his loud suits and gaudy jewellery.

The girls in the clubs liked Seamus: he was a big tipper. All they had to do was flash their tits in his general direction and he'd throw them a fiver. One night, as Seamus sat in his favourite club, which was just about to close, the human mountain that was Padraig O'Rourke, the resident senior bouncer, came in. He motioned to Seamus to come and join him at a table with four champagne glasses and a magnum of champagne on it.

Seamus wandered over. 'Fancy staying behind for a nightcap? I know someone who'd like to meet you.'

Seamus smiled. He guessed that the 'someone' Padraig was referring to was Carmel. She was one of Seamus's favourite girls.

Seamus sat down beside Padraig. Padraig was a monster. His body was sculpted to perfection from years of lifting free weights in Portlaoise Prison, where he had served seven years for membership of an illegal organisation. Padraig opened the champagne and filled two glasses. He called to the bar staff, telling them to go home, that he'd lock up.

Seamus smiled to himself. Four glasses meant four people . . . two women and two men . . . this was looking like a good night.

Seamus leaned back in his seat and relaxed. As he sipped his glass of bubbly, Carmel came out from the back room and walked over to their table. She looked lovelier than ever. She smiled at Seamus and kissed Padraig goodnight.

Seamus looked confused. Padraig laughed. 'Oh, I get it. You thought it was Carmel who wanted to meet you.'

'Well . . . I, I, I . . .'

'Sorry, mate. The person who wants to meet you is back there.'

Seamus followed Padraig's pointing finger. Two men appeared from behind the bar. One was about 60, and the other was young. As they made their way towards the table, Seamus noticed that the young one was carrying what looked like a toolbag. Seamus went to get up but felt Padraig's powerful grip on his arm. The old man sat down and poured himself a drink. The younger one stayed standing.

Seamus panicked. 'What's going on?'

No one answered.

The old man asked Padraig if they were alone. Padraig assured him that they were.

'Good.' He turned to Seamus and spoke in a whisper. 'I believe you have something that belongs to us.'

Seamus could feel his blood run cold. 'I don't know what you mean.'

The old man moved closer. 'We know.'

'Know what?'

The old man raised an eyebrow and before Seamus had a chance to say another word Padraig floored him with a right hook that would have made Lennox Lewis proud.

The old man looked down at him. 'Well, Seamus, let me explain . . . it's like this . . .'

He snapped his fingers and three men appeared from behind the stage curtain. Seamus recognised the badly beaten man in the middle. It was his co-op insider.

'I'm sorry, Seamus, I had no choice.'

Seamus shouted, 'What the fuck is he on about? I've never seen this guy before in my life.'

Padraig's boot connected with his face.

Seamus was dragged to his feet and pushed back into his chair, where one of the men started to wind a roll of masking tape around his body.

The old man continued. 'Let's cut to the chase. I know you did the co-op job.'

Seamus tried to protest.

'Gag him!' the old man barked at his men, before swiftly turning back to Seamus. 'That's for your own benefit, Seamus. I hate liars. Now, I know you did the co-op, but what I don't know is where you hid my money and who else was involved with you.'

The old man seemed to be enjoying himself. Seamus's insider was crying. Padraig stood to the left of Seamus and the toolbox man leaned against the bar.

'You planned the job very well, except for one small thing. You forgot to find out just whose money you were robbing. You see, it wasn't farmers' money you robbed, Seamus, it was Republican Army money. Now, I have neither the patience nor the inclination to go through hours of questioning with you, so I'm going to give it to you straight . . . you're in very serious trouble.'

He walked over to the tool man and tapped him on his shoulder. The man opened his bag and took out a battery-powered drill. He pulled out a ten-inch drill bit and began attaching it to the drill.

'James here is a genius with a drill, and I can assure you that he will get the information I need out of you. Now. The choice is yours. Do you want him to drill holes through every inch of your body, from your feet to your balls? Or are you going to save yourself a lot of pain and tell me what I want to know?'

Seamus struggled to get free.

'Are you ready to talk?'

Padraig ripped the tape from his mouth and pulled the rag from his mouth.

'I swear, I don't know . . .'

The old man snapped.

'Do him.'

Toolbag man began to drill holes in Seamus's feet. By the time he'd finished with the second foot, Seamus had fainted. Padraig slapped him in the face to bring him back around.

Seamus opened his eyes. The old man was inches from his face. 'I obviously haven't made myself clear. Now let me say it again. I will find out who your accomplices are. Even if I have to kill every single person you ever so much as spoke to, I will find out!'

He walked over to the toolbag and took out a handgun. He then moved towards the co-op insider, cocked the gun and shot him in the head.

'You are going to die, Seamus. The question is, do you want a quick death or a slow one? The choice is yours.'

Tommy was startled into consciousness by someone banging on the door.

'All right, all right, I'm coming!'

He jumped out of bed and crawled along the floor. He tapped the floorboards until one of them popped up. Tommy took out the Beretta and cocked it before he opened the door.

'Fuck you, Donie! What the hell are you do . . .' his words trailed off when he saw the state of his friend. 'What the fuck . . . ?'

Donie stood at the door wearing nothing but his trousers and a pair of socks. He was breathing heavily and his torso was covered in scrapes and bruises.

'Let me in,' Donie shouted, pushing Tommy out of the way. 'And close that fucking door.'

'What happened to you?'

Donie was moving frantically around the flat, peeping out the window and mumbling under his breath. He wasn't making any sense. Tommy grabbed him by the shoulders in an effort to make him stand still.

'What . . . the . . . fuck . . . is . . . going . . . on?'

'Haven't you heard?'

'Heard what?'

'Seamus . . .'

'What about Seamus?'

'Seamus is dead!'

'What? What do you mean, Seamus is dead? How? Where? When?'

'Jesus Christ, Tommy! Do you not watch the fucking news? It's only on every fucking channel, man!'

Tommy looked stunned. Donie turned on the telly and the RTE crime correspondent from Cork was standing on the banks of the Lee.

'The man is said to be in his early thirties and was a well-known, popular figure in the city.'

Tommy stared at Donie.

'The robbery!'

'Yep. We fucked up.'

'What do you mean, we fucked up? The job went perfect.'

'It has nothing to do with how it went. It's who we robbed.'

Tommy laughed. 'The co-op?'

'No, we didn't rob the fucking co-op. The money we robbed belonged to the fucking RA. It was fucking RA money!'

'You sure?'

Donie pointed at the television, shouting, 'Does that look like the work of the fucking co-op? Well, does it?'

He pointed to himself. 'They came round to my place and kicked the fucking door in. They tore the bedroom to pieces before they blasted the fucking room to shite.'

'How did you get out?'

'I was downstairs at the time, getting a glass of milk. I snuck out the back door and legged it across the fields until I got here. No one seen me.'

Tommy looked at him. 'Well, if they found you . . .'

'It's only a matter of time before they find you.'

Without another word, they went into the bedroom. Donie grabbed a shirt, jacket and shoes. Tommy grabbed his money and the guns. He threw a sawn-off gun and twenty grand across the bed to Donie. 'Take this and get the fuck out of here.'

Donie looked shocked. Tommy continued.

'They're onto us. We'll have a better chance if we split up.'

Donie grabbed the items Tommy had thrown on the bed and stuffed them into the hold-all. He hugged his friend and left. Tommy looked around the flat and decided that it would be best to leave everything as it was . . . as if he'd just nipped out for a few minutes. If the RA turned up and saw that the flat looked lived in, they'd probably decide to wait around for a while, thus buying Tommy some time.

Tommy left the flat and made his way through a housing estate. He saw a group of Romanians looking over a car. He approached them and offered a wad of notes . . . they didn't refuse.

Thirty minutes later, Tommy was speeding down the Dublin Road in the car. When he arrived in Dublin, he parked the car in Heuston train station, aware that within a few hours the untaxed, uninsured car would be towed away. He took a taxi to Dun Laoghaire Ferry Terminal and bought a one-way ticket to Holyhead.

Once Tommy had secured his ticket, he made his way to the bar, where he ordered a well-earned pint. When he sat down, he realised he still had the handgun in his pocket. A quick visit to the toilet and the gun was hidden in the cistern. Finally, he could relax. He ordered another pint.

Donie decided to take the train to Dublin. He stopped off at the Merchants Quay Shopping Centre to buy some much-needed clothes before making his way to the train station. While he waited on the platform, he noticed two men staring at him from the opposite side of the tracks.

'Oh, fuck,' he thought.

'Calm down,' he told himself. 'You're becoming paranoid. They're just two ordinary blokes waiting for a train.' But he couldn't keep his eyes off the men, whose eyes seemed to be following him as he walked up and down the platform. After what seemed like an eternity, the Cobh train arrived. As soon as the train stopped and the door opened, Donie decided to make his move. He ran towards the exit of the station. By the time the train had pulled away, he'd be well gone. He took the stairs three at a time and was waiting to cross the road before he heard the train pulling out. Just as he was about to cross the road, a car pulled up alongside him, and someone dragged Donie into the back. Before the car pulled away, the two men from the train station jumped in!

Dawn was breaking as the ferry docked in Holyhead. After a couple of pints, Tommy had fallen asleep and was unaware that the ferry had been delayed for hours due to bad weather. He stood back and let all the holidaymakers, who were still complaining about the delay, off first.

He made his way through customs without incident, and as he left the port he bought the *Irish Examiner* and tucked it under his arm. He boarded a train to London and, once he'd found a seat and settled himself comfortably, he opened the newspaper. It was full of the usual cheery news. High unemployment figures, brown envelope scandals, etc. Tommy almost missed the article in a side column on page three: 'Local man pulled from River Lee'.

No wonder people were starting to refer to Cork as 'the suicide capital of Ireland'. It seemed that every week another young person ended their life in the murky waters of the Lee. He searched the article for a name. Maybe he knew the family. When he found the name, his blood ran cold. Donie! The police were saying that the man had been murdered and that it looked like the work of dissident Republicans. Jaysus, Donie must have told them everything, otherwise he wouldn't be dead yet!

Tommy took the tube from Victoria station to Finsbury Park. Tommy knew the location well, he'd lived in London for eight years, but he would have to be careful. He'd have to stay away from his usual haunts. When he got off the tube, he headed down Blackstock Road. He was in the north of London, where he became one of the ten million people who pass through the streets and where no one gives a shite about anyone else.

He made his way to the Irish-owned Arsenal tavern. He knew he was taking a risk but he needed to score some weed and the Arsenal was the place to do it. He had only just sat down when a black guy approached him.

'Orwight, bro. Yah wanna score some weed?'

The guy's accent was a mixture of London and Jamaican. Tommy answered in the same accent. 'Yah, bro, gimme an eighth.'

They both laughed. The black guy took a small package from his shirt pocket and, slapping hands with Tommy, passed him the weed.

'Will you join me for a pint?' Tommy asked.

The black guy accepted, and by closing time Tommy knew all there was to know about Trevor.

Trevor offered Tommy his couch for the night and Tommy accepted.

The next morning, the pair went to a car auction in Walthamstow. They were standing drinking coffee when a Renault 25, 2.2 litre with a computerised brain, came under the hammer. Tommy knew he had to have it. Twenty minutes later, they were driving away in the Renault.

At Stansted Airport the CID Special Branch watched a grey-haired man come through the arrivals gate. He was met by a young couple who led him towards the car park. As they drove out of the car park, the grey-haired man was talking on his mobile phone, unaware that the helicopter overhead was trailing them. They drove down the M11 but turned off at the slip road for Tottenham.

They pulled up outside Merrion's Bar, an Irish pub that was also a guesthouse, unaware that their every move was being monitored by a British Telecom van that was parked across the road. The CID had second-guessed their movements. Danny Merrion was a Mayo man and a known Republican sympathiser, so it didn't take a genius to figure out this was where the trio would head.

Danny greeted his visitors warmly. He ordered drinks up for the couple before leading the old man upstairs to a bedroom.

'It's good to see you, Michael. I have everything arranged as requested, just call if you need anything else.'

'Thanks, Danny. I really appreciate your help.'

An hour later, when the old man had washed and changed his clothes, he held council in his room. Besides himself and Danny, there were three other men present. Michael filled them in on what had happened in Cork.

Danny nodded. 'So you want your money back?'

'Naturally. But I think you know by now, boys, that this has become personal. I want that scumbag begging me to kill him.'

Danny nodded to the other three men and they left the room. The old man looked at Danny.

'Will they find him?'

Danny laughed. 'If he's in London, they'll find him.'

The BT van had recorded the whole conversation. Tommy's details were circulated to every police station in the Greater London area. The head of the CID surveillance team knew that they had to find this Tommy character before the IRA did, if they wanted to knock the London operation on the head.

When Tommy dropped Trevor off at his flat, he handed him a wad of cash. 'Thanks for all your help, bro.'

'No probs. If you ever need anything, just give me a call.' He handed Tommy his phone number.

Tommy drove away and headed to Broadwater Farm, where he was to meet a homie who Trevor had said would fix him up with a gun. Tommy knew he was taking a risk by trusting Trevor, but right now he didn't have much choice. Broadwater Farm was a black housing estate with a big reputation. It had been at the centre of the race riots in the early '80s, when a white policeman had been hacked to death while attempting to make an arrest.

Not much had changed on the estate in the twenty years since the riots. As Tommy drove through, a group of black kids who couldn't have been more than sixteen came towards him. One kid stood in the middle of the road, forcing Tommy to stop.

Tommy stopped the car and rolled down the window. 'Is Winston around?'

The kid who stood in front of the car called to the others. 'Eh, mon, this blood clot 'ere be looking for Winston.'

Tommy smiled at the kid's overdone accent.

There was a stand-off. Tommy knew that word of his arrival – and who he was looking for – was going all around the estate. This was one of those situations where he had to be patient. The gang surrounded the car as Tommy, trying to act casual, tapped on the steering wheel in time to the radio. Eventually, a tall, well-built Rastafarian opened the passenger door and got into the car. Tommy and the Rasta touched fists as a mark of street respect.

'Why yoh look for Winston, mun?'

'Trevor told me he could supply me with what I need.'

His accent became less Jamaican, more London.

'Trevor, eh? Well, if Trevor sent you, you must be cool. I'm Winston, what can I do you for?'

'I need a gun and some ammo.'

'Not the kind of thing I have to hand.'

'But you can get them?'

The Rastafarian laughed. 'I can get anything at a price. Come back at two with a grand.'

Tommy arrived back at two and the deal went off without a hitch.

The next thing on his list was to find a place to stay. He found a small flat in Edmonton, where he was asked for a deposit and a month's rent up front before he would be allowed to move in. He paid in euros. He now had somewhere to lie low while he waited for this mess to blow over.

Danny and the old man passed the time by playing pool. But they weren't really concentrating. Every time the door opened or the phone rang, their heads swung round. Eventually the call they were waiting for came through. It was the barman from the Arsenal Tavern. He told Danny that Tommy had been in the pub and that he had left with one of the regulars, a black guy, a weed dealer who never strayed too far from the Arsenal.

Half an hour later, the old man and Danny were still playing pool, but in the Arsenal Tavern. When Trevor entered the pub, the barman nodded to him. Trevor walked over to the jukebox and pumped coins into it until Bob Marley's 'Three Little Birds' was blasting around the pub.

The old man caught Trevor's eye and called him over. Trevor, smelling money, didn't hesitate. 'Wazup, man?'

'I'm looking for my son. His name is Tommy.'

'There's a lotta Tommys an' Paddys in this neck o dah woods, mun.'

'This one has only just arrived . . . fresh off the boat,' the old man said as he pushed forty pounds across the table.

One look into the old man's eyes and Trevor knew he wasn't dealing with a grieving father.

'Ah's sorry, mun, I can't help you.'

As Trevor went to stand up, the old man grabbed his arm.

'Oh, but I think you can help me.'

Trevor felt the barrel of a gun dig into his side.

Across the bar, a slight girl drinking a tomato juice listened intently to the conversation. Her fellow officers waited outside.

Danny made a phone call and within minutes the three men from the earlier meeting arrived on the scene.

Trevor told them everything he knew about Tommy. But he couldn't give them an address because he didn't have one. The old man wasn't impressed.

'Take him outside. Maybe the fresh air will jog his memory.'

Tommy was furious with himself. What had he been thinking of, handing all that cash to a London real estate agent? He was supposed to be lying low, not flashing foreign money all over the place! He would have to be more careful. The sooner he changed the money into sterling the better.

He had a shower and changed into fresh clothes before heading to his new local, The Red Lion. The pub was heaving with English people, with not an Irish accent to be heard. Tommy was happy about this, along with the fact that the local police station was only fifty yards away, so a lot of coppers drank here too. No con in his right mind would come within a mile of this place. Tommy checked the handgun in his inside pocket before sitting down and opening up his newspaper. At closing time, he decided to pay Trevor a visit.

When Trevor stumbled back into the Arsenal Tavern, he was bleeding heavily. The barman phoned for an ambulance. Having tortured Trevor for an hour, the old man was finally convinced that he was telling the truth, and that he didn't know where Tommy was.

As the old man and his crew made their way back to the Merrion, they were followed closely by the police. When they arrived at the Merrion's car park, they were surrounded.

'Armed police. Stay by the car and do not move. I repeat, do not move.'

Danny Merrion, who had travelled back earlier, stood at the pub's back door and shouted to the old man to come in. The IRA men went for their guns, but before they had a chance to reach them the car park exploded in a hail of automatic gunfire.

The old man ran for the pub, but as Danny went to close the door a bullet hit him in the face, splattering blood everywhere. The police continued firing as they stood over the four bodies.

The old man slammed the door shut and ran towards the basement. He knew that every base should be fitted with an escape route. Merrion had paid attention to his training and, as the police were hammering down the door, the old man was crawling through a three-foot by three-foot tunnel that led him to the other side of the road. He was on his way to the tube station by the time the police got into the basement. He would have to get out of England tonight. Tommy and the money would have to wait for another day.

Tommy tried Trevor's flat but got no reply. His mobile was switched off too. Tommy thought this was strange, considering Trevor was a drug-dealer. He headed for the

Arsenal Tavern, but as he reached it someone coming along the road told him to stay away.

'Old Bill, mate. They're swarming the place.'

'What happened?'

The stranger told him that a black guy had been beaten up by a group of Irish boys.

'Probably had something to do with drugs. The black dude must have pissed on their patch.'

Tommy agreed and headed off back to his flat.

That night the news carried a full report on the deaths of an IRA gang who were about to go on a killing spree in North London. They produced a photofit of one of the IRA men who had escaped, and Tommy's heart skipped a beat as he recognised the photo as that of the old man from the co-op. He knew now that he had been the intended target, and that whatever chance he'd once had of talking to the IRA was now well and truly gone!

A year later, Tommy still slept with his gun under his pillow. He had used his money from the robbery to buy into the drug scene and was building up a good network across Europe. He had bought a detached house in Waltham Abbey on the outskirts of Essex and was driving a Range Rover. But no matter how hard he tried to maintain a low profile, word still managed to get back to Cork that Tommy was doing very well in England.

He started to get crank hang-up calls on his business phone and, despite the fact that he changed the phone every three days, the calls would start up again within an hour of changing it. Tommy knew deep down that someone was toying with him.

Then one night the call he had been expecting for over a year came. It was from a woman who told him she was calling on behalf of a mutual friend.

'Our mutual friend is willing to accept the return of his money plus an interest and inconvenience payment of four hundred thousand pounds sterling.'

Tommy tried to explain that 'their mutual friend' had already got most of his money back from the two other members of the gang that he'd visited in Cork.

'I'm sorry, Tommy. This offer is not up for discussion. However, I can guarantee you that if you do exactly what is asked of you, you will not be killed.'

The woman then told him that he had a week to return to Cork where he would be met by a volunteer who knew him by sight, then the phone went dead.

Tommy's legs gave way, and as he sat down and poured himself a large whiskey he felt his whole world was falling apart. Tommy called in every favour he was owed from his connections in the drug-smuggling world. He'd already made three times the amount he'd got from the co-op robbery, but had invested it wisely in small businesses and real estate: a good choice for his retirement fund, but unless he got his hands on the money he owed the IRA he wouldn't be around for his retirement.

It took him five days to get the cash he needed and it was now sitting in an oversized hold-all on his kitchen floor. There was no way he was risking bringing the money into Ireland. Apart from the risk of having to go through customs, he still wasn't sure that the IRA weren't just setting him up. He addressed the parcel of money and sent it with DHL, who would deliver it to Cork General Post Office.

As Tommy left his house and headed towards the airport, he found himself stopping at the Catholic church. And for the first time in his adult life, he prayed. He prayed that his mother and father would be looking over him as he dealt with the IRA. This was the first time in Tommy's life that he had felt real fear, and he smiled at the irony of it all. For a couple of minutes he realised how his street-dealing 'employees' must feel every day of their lives.

Tommy thought about the life he had in London – the money, the fancy cars, the houses and the women – but none of it mattered now. Every night he awoke from his nightmares in a sweat, the old man's piercing eyes a constant reminder of all that had happened. In his dreams the old man was standing over the bodies of Tommy's two friends.

Tommy parked in the airport's long-term car park. Everything went according to plan. Travelling first class sure had its advantages, and he was through customs in a flash. When he reached the arrivals hall, he turned on his mobile phone; it rang straight away.

'Fuck,' he thought, scanning the crowds. 'Someone must be watching me.'

'Yeah?'

The woman who had arranged the meeting spoke.

'Go to the taxi rank and take the taxi with the shamrock on the roof sign.'

The phone went dead. Tommy muttered to himself.

'Fucking typical. They've probably hired a fucking leprechaun with an AK47 machine gun to bump me off.'

He walked out of the airport and made his way to the taxi rank. He spotted the taxi with the shamrock and got in. The driver looked like any other taxi man, and he didn't say a word. He simply adjusted his rear-view mirror and kept his eye on Tommy as he drove. Eventually Tommy had had enough. He leaned forward and shouted at the driver, 'Listen, mate, if I'd known you'd fancied me so much I'd have brought a photo for you to keep. You fucking faggot!'

'Fuck off, you little shit! And watch your fucking mouth. I'm not one of your drugged-up gofers. You shout at me once more and I'll do you, do you hear me?'

Tommy sat back, laughing. The driver continued his rant. 'Who the fuck are you laughing at? I'm warning y . . .'

Tommy laughed louder.

'You know, I think I preferred you when you were quiet.'

Tommy recognised the area. They were in a small village called Carrigaline on the way to Crosshaven. Tommy's money was on Crosshaven. It was a little seaside town notorious for its IRA sympathisers. It was the kind of area where robberies went unreported because the locals always took care of their own affairs.

The taxi driver's phone rang. 'Yeah? Yeah, he's here.' He looked in the rear-view mirror. Tommy caught his eye and blew him a kiss. 'But I don't think he's got the package with him.'

The driver handed the phone to Tommy. 'They want to talk to you.'

Tommy took the phone and was surprised to hear a male voice on the other end.

'Where's the money?'

'It's safe.'

'That's not what I asked.'

'I have to safeguard my life here, mate.'

'I am not your mate and this deal is non-negotiable. Now tell the driver where to go.'

Tommy handed the phone back to the driver.

'Slight change of plan, follow my directions.'

Tommy directed the driver off the main dual carriageway and through the side streets of Cork. When they had passed the same pub three times from three different directions, the driver knew that Tommy was taking the piss. His glare was enough to convince Tommy that the joke had gone far enough.

'OK, head for the GPO.'

Tommy entered the post office through the main door.

The driver tooted on his car horn, and when Tommy looked around he pointed to his watch. 'Go fuck yourself,' Tommy thought, as he strolled to the counter. Of course, on the day when Tommy didn't care how long the assistant took she became Miss Efficient, and less than five minutes later Tommy was walking through the doors again with the parcel.

The driver put the parcel into the boot of the car and drove towards Crosshaven. They were making good time – too good for Tommy's liking! They drove to an eighteenth-century coastal fort that the Irish Navy and the Provisionals used as a training ground. Tommy followed the driver through endless tunnels and stairways. He knew this was the kind of place where you could kill someone without any risk of being caught.

He was starting to sweat profusely. His hands became so wet that he lost his grip and dropped the parcel. As he bent down to pick it up, the driver gave him a kick, knocking him to the ground.

'You stupid cunt!'

Tommy went to retaliate but the driver pointed a gun to his head.

'Go on . . . make my day.'

A voice came out of the shadows. 'Leave it.'

Tommy stayed on the ground. He couldn't see the faces of the three men coming towards him, but as they got nearer he recognised the old man. The other two wore balaclavas. All three of them were armed. Tommy was praying that the 'People's Army' would be good to their word and not kill him.

The old man stepped forward. 'Is it all here?'

Tommy, despite his fear, didn't falter. 'If you don't trust me, count it.'

The barrel of the old man's gun connected with Tommy's

forehead. 'Don't get smart with me. Do you have any idea how much trouble you've caused us? Four of our best men died because of you. We had to cancel operations in Britain, halt the war, because of you.'

One of the masked men added, 'Not to mention the problems the loss of nine hundred grand caused us.'

Tommy wiped blood from his forehead. 'You got most of that back when you killed my friends.'

The old man kicked him. 'Shut the fuck up.'

He cocked his gun. Tommy eyeballed him.

'I thought you Provos were men of honour. I'm giving you a million pounds and you're still not happy.'

'I told you to shut the fuck up.'

He put his finger on the trigger. One of the masked men stepped forward.

'Stop.'

The old man hesitated.

'That's an order.'

The masked man leaned down and held Tommy's face in a vice-like grip.

'I want you to tell me everything. Leave nothing out . . . because believe me, this is a matter of life and death.'

Tommy found himself reliving every detail of the co-op robbery. The only time the man in the balaclava spoke was to ask why they'd chosen the co-op in the first place.

'We were told the job was a piece of cake,' Tommy answered.

The masked man paced up and down. The old man hissed that Tommy was a fucking liar and they needed to waste him. The masked man came to Tommy again.

'What happened in London?'

'I don't know anything other than what I heard and saw on the news.' He looked into the man's eyes. 'I swear.'

The man swung round to face the old man.

'I thought you said he'd set you up?'

The old man was sweating and trembling. The man who had stood in the shadows moved forward and, shoving the old man against the wall, he held a gun under his chin. The first masked man punched a number into his mobile phone.

'I'm going to sort this out once and for all.'

He spoke quietly into the phone before turning to the taxi driver.

'You, get the hell out of here. I'll call when we need you . . .' He looked at Tommy and the old man. 'This could take a few hours.'

Tommy didn't like the sound of this. The man turned to them.

'When that phone rings again, I'll be given information. That information will dictate which one of you walks out of here tonight and which one doesn't.'

Tommy looked over at the old man. 'Are you happy now?' Tommy shouted to him. 'Was it worth it? Skimming off the top like that?!'

'Shut up, you! You're dead, do you hear? Dead!'

The second masked man put his finger to his lips.

'Ssssh.'

Tommy looked over at the old man and wondered how this pathetic, snivelling little shit had caused him such fear for so long.

The minutes ticked slowly by. It seemed like hours had passed before the phone rang. The balaclava man looked from Tommy to the old man, as he mumbled into the phone. Eventually he hung up. He walked towards Tommy, gun in hand.

'Get up.'

Tommy's legs turned to lead. The man dragged him to his feet.

'I said . . . get up!'

He stared straight into Tommy's eyes.

'You are one lucky bastard. I want you to get out of here now! And I don't mean this village . . . I mean this country. Don't ever come back because if you do, I will kill you.'

Tommy didn't need to be told twice. He ran like fuck until he reached daylight. As he walked out into the sunshine, he heard the sound of a bullet in the distance. The shamrock taxi pulled up beside him.

'Get in. I've to make sure you don't miss your plane.'

Three hours later, Tommy arrived in Stansted.

The first thing he did when he got home was pour himself a large stiff drink and put on Billy Joel's 'Piano Man'. As the music started, he sat back in his luxurious leather armchair and toasted his dead mates.

It had been a hectic time when he'd honestly thought he was going to die, but he hadn't. He looked around and let out a long sigh. He still had his profitable business, and the trouble was off his back. He closed his eyes and slept the most peaceful sleep he'd had in over a year.

Raving Mad – by Fatboy

It's the early eighties and me and my mates are mad into reggae. We'd get a bit of hash and sit back and listen to the world according to Bob Marley. We'd do all kinds of stuff with the hash: five-skinners; bongs; waterfalls; pipes; and my favourite, blowbacks. You light a spliff and a mate takes the lit end in his mouth while you take the other end . . . he blows back as you inhale. Talk about being fucked up!

The worst thing about blowbacks is when it's your turn to blow. Odds on, a few hot ashes would fall onto your tongue . . . ah, the pain of it. When that happened, the person with the burnt tongue would jump up screaming and kicking and the rest of us would roll around the place laughing. Of course, if you asked for another blowback after that, you'd be told straight out to fuck off!

By the late eighties, the big new sensation was acid. Acid had hit England big-time and the raves were causing the English police serious headaches. The coverage shown on the evening news was obviously meant to shock, but for me it had the opposite effect . . . I wanted to go to England.

Dublin was catching on . . . slowly. There were a few clubs starting to play rave music, but they still insisted on playing slow sets and serving beer.

Me and my mates got into acid, big-style. We'd head down

to Oliver Bond flats. You could get any trips you wanted in Oliver Bond: yeng-yang, strawberries, and the strongest of them all, microdots. Microdots were the only tabs not on paper. They resembled the flint from a lighter . . . and fucked up your head for hours. After getting stoned, we'd head to a club.

The first thing that hit you when you entered a club was the heat. Then, as the drugs kicked in, you'd see all the colours of the rainbow floating before your eyes. In order to keep the bouncers off our backs, we'd buy a round of drinks, then we'd find a quiet corner where we'd smoke a few joints. It seemed as if we took it in turns to go mad on the gear, for every weekend at least one of us would go on a mad one and not be seen for days.

In 1990, The Olympic opened, and it quickly became the in place. It was great. The bouncers let anybody in. It didn't matter whether you were dressed in a tracksuit and runners or a suit. Once you paid the seven quid, you were in. The place would be heaving with the beat of the music and the sound of two thousand people dancing on the floor. And the beautiful smell of drugs was everywhere.

I found a quiet corner, as some mates went off to score XTC. I wanted some too but just sat back and enjoyed watching everyone have fun. I'd never seen anything like it. The lasers had me in a trance, so much so that I didn't even notice my mates coming back until one of them slapped me in the face. Pissing themselves laughing at the state of me, they give me a small white tablet with a white dove on one side of it. This tab has set me back twenty-five quid! My mates are telling me not to take any more than a half, seeing as it's my first time to take it. I head to the bar and buy a coke. I swallow the half and it leaves a bad taste in my mouth, so I drink some coke to take away the taste and then I head back to my mates and smoke a few joints.

There's a strange feeling coming over my body. The hairs on the back of my neck are standing up, and my jaws are going like the clappers. I chew some Orbit chewing gum to try and control my jaws, I'm sweating like a pig. I get a weird feeling like someone has walked on my grave. My friends notice what's happening and tell me to get on the dance floor. I push my way onto the floor and am greeted by a thousand like-minded people. We are all happy and hugging and in love. I am hugging and kissing my way from one group to another, when suddenly there's an absolute stunner standing in front of me. She puts out her arms and is hugging me like a long-lost lover, her fabulous tits melting into me. She starts kissing me, running her fingers up and down my back. I don't know what's happening here, but I do know I'm liking it. I start rubbing her too. She lets go of me and starts dancing, shaking her hips and ass, all sexy like. The music is pumping really fast; the strobe lighting is flashing, making everyone look as if they are moving in slow motion. The DJ puts on another record and the whole place goes crazy. This bird grabs my hands and squeezes them so hard that I feel a rush coming all over my body. She tells me to do the same to her and, I swear, I could have snapped her little fingers. The ecstasy tabs have me feeling on top of the world. She turns her back on me but still has a hold of my hands. I can't believe my luck. The lights go out and the smoke puffs out, engulfing everybody. It feels cold on my skin. Then the laser beams kick in. At first it's just one tiny beam, then hundreds, getting wider and wider, turning into a tunnel, and with all the smoke floating in the air I feel as if I'm being sucked in. I'm on top of the world. I feel a piss coming on so I tell the girl to wait and I head to the toilet.

When I get to the toilet, the sweat is running out of me and my clothes are soaking. I'm fucking freezing but there is steam coming off my body and I can feel the goose pimples all over me. I look in the mirror. My pupils are huge. All around me, people are jumping up and down hugging each other, rolling joints, sniffing Vics and poppers. I have half an E left. I'm feeling in my pockets, starting to panic, thinking I've lost it when suddenly I find it lurking in the corner of my tracksuit bottoms. My hands are shaking, I walk over to the sink to get a drink of water. I put my hand on the tap and turn it . . . shite! My fucking ecstasy tab falls into the sink! Fuck, fuck, fuck . . . I'm screaming and kicking the sink. Two blokes approach and tell me to chill. I tell them what's happened. They smile and the bigger of the two puts his hand in his pocket and pulls out a bag of ecstasy tabs.

'Here, have one. On the house.'

I swallow the tab, not bothering with water. The smaller bloke puts his hand into his pocket and pulls out a bag of coke. The three of us squeeze into a toilet cubicle, where we snort a few lines and talk a mile a minute. I start to feel the effects of the coke . . . it feels fucking great! No one can touch me.

Suddenly, I remember the bird outside. I say my goodbyes and leave the toilet. The heat hits me like a slap in the face. I'm looking all around but I can't see her. The ecstasy is swimming all around my head and body. I'm more stoned than ever before. I bump into my mates and they ask where the fuck I was. I blurt out everything that has happened and they piss themselves laughing. They're with their birds, and I don't need this. I slip off by myself to a quiet corner and smoke spliffs. People keep asking me if I'm OK. I just wish they'd all fuck off and leave me alone to enjoy my buzz. I look at my watch; it's time to head before it becomes too mad. I go upstairs to get my coat, watching my step because the floor is wet with sweat, and there she is, my bird. I can't believe it; she turns and screams, running to me with outstretched arms, asking where the fuck I've been.

We collect our coats and she brings me over to meet her friends. They all want to chat. I just want sex. I ask her if she wants to come to a party. I know all my mates are heading to Bumbler's house. Bumbler's house is a crazy fucked-up shit-hole where we all sit around doing drugs.

We arrive at Bumbler's house. The bedroom lights are on and the music is pumping. We walk into the gaff and Bumbler asks if anyone wants a cup of tea. We all say yes. 'Ah, no. Fuck off. There's too many of yous. I'd have to boil the kettle twice!'

We're running low on hash. The lads know I have a kilo hidden in the field at the back of the estate and ask me to go and get it. I ask my bird if she wants to come with me. As we head out the door, all the lads start roaring. They know what I have in mind. As we walk through my estate, I can see the look of shock on her face, as she looks around at all the graffiti and the burned-out cars. We get to the field and sit down. She starts telling me how much she loves the sunrise and I agree.

'Yeah, it's nice.'

I put my hands around her waist and we kiss. I get my hands on her tits and she starts rubbing her hand up the inside of my leg. Bingo! I'm on top of her and we're ripping each other's clothes off. It's amazing. When we'd finished, we just lay there, staring up at the dawn sky. We smoke a joint and I don't want this moment to ever end. But I know it will, like everything good in life. We get dressed and head back towards Bumbler's with the hash. As we're walking back, I hear the familiar sound of a stolen car skidding up and down the estate. We sit on a wall and watch the car do handbrake after handbrake. She turns to me and tells me she's never before had a night like we've just had. I smile and agree, but in my mind I wish she would go.

All I want now is a spin in the stolen car.

The Model – by D.G.

Eight-thirty in the morning and I woke up to the usual infernal racket.

'Right, lads! Breakfast time! Up, up, up!!'

'Right, up the fuck.'

That was the worst thing about Loughran House; they just didn't let you sleep. I mean, it's ten times better than manky Mountjoy, but at the end of the day it's still a prison – no locked doors, but prison nonetheless. And, like in all prisons, they seemed to get great satisfaction in getting us up early.

'I won't tell you again . . . out of your room, now!'

I was always bad at getting up early, but next to my roommate, John, I was an early bird. We'd only been sharing for three days but I liked him, even if he was a lazy bastard.

He was still in bed as I left the room and headed down the hall to join the pandemonium that was breakfast. Screws were roaring for the stragglers to get a move on, while the prisoners were all chat, even though they hadn't showered yet.

'This is your last warning . . . out of them beds, now!'

I looked back and saw John staggering out of the room and down the landing like a Saturday-night drunk. If I hadn't been in the room with him all night, I'd have sworn the fucker had got drink in. John was always like this in the mornings. His eyes were never fully opened until he had a couple of cups of tea inside him.

Collecting the muck they called breakfast, I found a table and sat down.

Loughran House was in the arsehole of County Cavan, a minimum-security prison just on the border of Fermanagh. Two fences surrounded the House, but inside life was as normal as any institution would allow it to be. There were big fields to play sports on and a couple of tennis courts, and we weren't locked in at night.

As we sat in silence eating our breakfast, Cody and Tommy joined us. The crew was gathered. I was serving eighteen months for fraud. Cody was doing eighteen months for a whole load of minor offences. He was one of the most relaxed guys I knew. Nothing ever fazed him and you could talk to him about anything and he never got annoyed. We'd been calling him Cody for so long that none of us could remember his real name. In fact, I couldn't even remember how he had become part of our crew; it just seemed to happen. He was a bit clumsy but sound.

Tommy was a different kettle of fish, no pun intended – he was a salmon poacher, you see. A big fucker, he'd battered two guards and got eighteen months for it. Tommy was a big bloke and no one messed with him.

And then there was John. We all felt sorry for John. I mean, we'd all got fair sentences (not that you'd let anyone know that), but poor old John hadn't – he'd got twelve months for robbing and cutting up a bike! Hardly Ronnie Biggs, now. He got a terrible slagging from the other lads over it.

The worst thing about prison is the boredom. Every day is the same. It's regimental. You could either go to school or to the workshop in order to pass the hours until dinner-time.

Over dinner, things would liven up a bit. There was always plenty of slagging going on. We slagged each other about anything and everything. We were all mad about football, cars and women, though not necessarily in that order. John was always getting slagged about this mysterious girlfriend he was supposed to have. Because he was relatively new to the prison, the mysterious girlfriend hadn't written to him yet, so the lads kept saying she was a figment of his imagination.

'I'm telling you, I do have a girlfriend. She's English!'

'Yeah, right, that's handy. She can hardly visit if she lives in England.'

'Her name's Sandy.'

'Are you sure you don't mean Sammy? Have you anything you'd like to tell us?'

'Fuck off! I'm telling you, she's a beaut. Five foot four, small and beautiful, with dark skin.'

'A nigger. Your girlfriend's a nigger?'

'Half-caste.'

We were all falling around the place laughing; John got up and stormed off.

That evening, we sat around in Tommy's room just buzzing off each other. John was still in a strop and refused to talk about his girlfriend.

'Just yous wait till I get a letter. That'll prove to yous that she's real and not a figment of my imagination!'

It was coming close to Christmas and I think we all secretly wanted a girlfriend. Christmas is the shittiest time of the year to be in prison. All you think about is the wild parties that your mates are having and how easy it is for people to forget all about you when they have a social life to look forward to. Sure, your mates would make their dutiful Christmas visit and then they'd head off to enjoy the festive spirit. At least if you had a girlfriend, you could look forward

Leabharlanna Poiblí Chathair Bhaile Átha Cliath

Dublin City Public Libraries

to getting a phone call on Christmas Day. I know it doesn't sound like much but it's better than nothing. Tommy was married and was getting out on temporary release for the Christmas period; the rest of us had nothing. However, we had hatched a plan to get ourselves legless on Christmas Day so that the day would pass as quickly as possible and would be over before we knew it.

Cody had a contact who was going to get us some hash, and I was getting the whiskey and vodka in. We'd have to hide the booze in the grounds but I wasn't worried about that, I was determined to be out of my tree when Santa came calling.

Next morning, the usually bleary-eyed John came running down the landing full of the joys of life and waving a letter in the air.

'See . . . see! What do you think of this?'

I'd forgotten all about our slagging match.

'What? What are you on about?'

'Her!'

Tommy got annoyed.

'Who?'

'Sandy. This letter is from Sandy!'

For the next hour, we had to listen to every boring detail of Sandy's life.

Sandy went shopping.

Yipee!

Sandy washed the car.

Whoopee doo!

Sandy went to see her ma.

God, we were so jealous.

All he was short of telling us was when Sandy had a shite. I was disgusted. After all, the whole point of letters was to supply information and wanking material. Sandy had supplied neither.

Tommy and Cody were lucky. At least they didn't have to hear the letter over and over again; they were able to escape back to their own room. I had to endure John laughing at all the stupid stuff she told him and then, when he insisted on reading it to me (again), I was supposed to fall about the place laughing too.

'Hey, you?'

'Yes?'

'Would you like to see a photo of Sandy? I didn't want to show it to the others 'cause they'll only take the piss.'

I smiled to myself. She must be a right dog. I had to get a look at her so I could tell the lads. 'Sure, yeah, why not?'

He went over to his bag and started rooting in it.

'She must be bad if you have to hide her photo.'

He walked over and handed me it.

'Jaysus.'

I couldn't believe it, she was actually good-looking.

'So it is true, John.'

'What?'

'That good-looking women do find ugly men attractive.'

He snatched the photo back.

'Ah, fuck off.'

We laughed.

'Ah, no, seriously, John, she's a good-looking bird.'

'Thanks.'

'Does she have any mates?'

'Well, yes, actually, she has one friend.'

'Really, what's her name?'

'Michelle.'

'Nice name. Is she a dog? Good-looking birds like to hang around with ugly birds. It makes them look better.'

'I don't know. She could be, I've never met her. Sandy said she's a glamour model.'

A model, I thought. Jaysus, she must be good-looking then.

I knew that if Cody heard about Michelle, he'd start writing to her, so I decided to say nothing. That night, while John replied to Sandy, I started my masterpiece to Michelle.

'All right, Michelle, I'm a friend of John's . . .'

An hour later, I was still staring at those eight words. This writing to a total stranger lark was a lot harder than I'd thought it would be. Eventually I finished the letter. I didn't know what I'd written, but it'd covered a full foolscap page. John legged it down and posted it straight away.

When Cody found out about my letter, he started slagging me, saying she probably had black eyes and curly teeth.

'She's a model.'

'A model for a ride with a bag over her head.'

We all laughed.

'Well, John said she's a glamour model.'

'What's that?'

'I don't know, but Sandy says she's nice.'

Cody laughed. 'You're fucked now. When a bird says her mate is nice, she's usually talking about her personality!'

I had to agree, it definitely wasn't looking good.

Soon we got fed up talking about 'the model' and things went back to normal. Tommy was all excited about getting out for Christmas but guilty because we would be left behind. We told him not to be stupid because we'd all be gone given half the chance.

Myself and Cody took up photography classes to pass the time. We took photos of birds and plants, but soon got bored so we moved on to portraits. I figured I had drawn the short straw when it was decided that Cody would take my photo, but it turned out OK. I had to say that, given my ugly mug, he'd done well.

One of the screws called me, saying he had a letter for me. He was sniggering as he handed it to me. I felt like telling him to fuck off, but decided against it. I sat down with the lads and opened the letter up. A photo fell out: it was Michelle. I don't know what I had been expecting but it wasn't this. The photo showed her lying on a bed, stark naked. Her legs were spread wide and she had the most beautiful pair of tits cupped in her hands. She looked as if she was about to suck her nipples with those beautiful lips that at that moment were smiling at me. She was fucking gorgeous. Think blonde, blue eyes, perfect size ten and you're on the right track. The lads couldn't believe it either. No wonder the screw was sniggering, no doubt they'd all had a good look at my Michelle.

Cody was drooling.

'You jammy bastard.'

'Keep it down,' I whispered, grabbing the photo from him. 'I don't want everyone knowing about her.'

'Hey, John. Has Sandy got any more friends?'

'I thought you didn't believe there was a Sandy?'

'Yeah, well, I do now.'

I didn't want the others reading my letter so I legged it outside. I knew they'd go to my room looking for me. They'd never think that I'd be outside in the fucking sub-zero temperatures.

She had lovely handwriting, and told me that she was originally from Stockport but now lived in Manchester. She had a daughter and had been modelling since she was seventeen (five years). She said that she had wanted to send an ordinary picture but Sandy had insisted that she send one of her glamour shots. Thank you, Sandy.

Regardless of what she looked like, she actually sounded like a nice girl, real down to earth. She asked me if I would like her to call me. Would I ever?!

I ran up to my room and started on my reply. I decided to send her the picture Cody had taken of me. I checked the date – 19 December 1996. Shite, I thought. There was no way I'd get a reply before Christmas. Fuck the Christmas post.

Michelle was the talk of the prison. Fellas I hardly knew and never talked to were asking for a look at my girlfriend. I decided to try and put her out of my mind and concentrate on matters in hand. We had Christmas contraband to organise.

I was walking back to my room when a screw called me. Fuck, they've found the whiskey. It turned out, though, that I had a phone call.

That was strange. I wasn't expecting anyone.

I answered the phone and the sweetest voice I had ever heard answered back. It was Michelle. She seemed nervous at first but she soon relaxed and started telling me what she was wearing, right down to the colour of her G-string.

I found myself telling her all about myself, right down to why I was in prison. I told her that the other guy I worked with had done a runner to England and I wished I had gone with him. She said, 'I'm glad you didn't.'

'Why?'

''Cause if you had, we would never have met.'

Eventually I had to hang up, but she promised that she'd ring again after Christmas. Who said Christmas inside wasn't good? This was going to be the best Christmas ever.

On 23 December, I met Cody staggering up the stairs. It was obvious from the state of him that the bastard had hit our drink early. I panicked; I had visions of a dry Christmas! I asked him where John was and he told me he was outside. I found John flaked out in a field, drunk as a skunk, halfway to hypothermia. I picked him up and carried the fucker back inside before he froze to death.

Luckily no one saw us, so our stash was safe. Cody and John had only managed to down half a bottle of vodka before they dropped. I took the half-bottle of vodka and called in on another fella I knew. 'Christmas has come early,' I told him. Together we got completely rat-arsed.

The next three days are nothing but a hazy memory. I can vaguely remember Cody and John joining us, and I must have slept in my own bed at night because if I hadn't the screws would have been onto me. Anyway, who cares . . . it was all a beautiful, drink-induced blur.

Life returned to normal, when on 28 December I woke up with the mother of all hangovers. Even the painkillers needed painkillers. Cody came in.

'Come on, let's go for a walk to clear our heads.'

'Cody, I can't even feel my head, never mind clear it!' I said as I struggled to get out of bed.

But Cody was right. The crisp air did help to clear my head, and slowly, very, very slowly, I began to feel normal again.

'So you're going to see Michelle?'

'What?'

'When you were on the phone the other night, you told her you were going to escape so's you could go and see her.'

I nearly shit myself; I didn't remember a thing.

'Fuck off, Cody, that's not funny.'

'I'm only telling you what you told her.'

'Jaysus Christ! I'm a fucking eejit when I'm drunk.'

'Aren't we all?'

'Yeah, but at least you don't go blabbing all over the prison. Christ, if the screws get wind of this, I'm fucked!'

'Relax, would you? You didn't blab all over the prison. You just told me and John what you'd been saying to her on the phone, like you always do . . . like we all do.'

I stood still, trying to remember.

'Jaysus, the only reason I'm saying anything, is because I want to ask you something.'

'What?'

117

'Well, if you are planning an escape . . .'

I cut him off. 'For fuck sake, Cody, I'm not planning anything . . .'

'Yeah, yeah, right. But if you are planning anything, make sure you let me know.'

When we came back from our walk, we saw that Tommy was back.

Naturally we all wanted to know every detail of what Christmas had been like on the outside. He got a great laugh when we told him about our exploits. We were having a great laugh, buzzing off each other, when a screw appeared and told me I had a phone call. I could hear the others shouting after me as I walked down the hall to receive it.

Michelle was in great form and we chatted for ages before she asked the question I'd been dreading.

'Well, when are you coming over to see me?'

'Michelle, you know I can't come to England. That was just the drink talking.'

'Oh, really,' she teased. 'So are you saying you don't want to see me?'

'No, no. Nothing like that.'

'Then come on. I'm here now in just my bra and knickers . . .'

'Ah, don't . . .'

'On the bed . . .'

'Michelle that's not fair . . .'

'So hornyyyyyyyyyyyy . . .'

When I got back to the room, the others cheered.

'Well, how is the English nympho?'

I closed the door.

'Right, lads, listen up . . . we've got an escape to plan.'

The next morning, we started to plan the escape. A new three-million-pound security system had recently been installed into Loughran House, and there were cameras everywhere. No one had escaped since the new system had been installed. This new system would make things difficult, but in a way it also gave us an added thrill. I mean, if – no, *when* – we escaped, we'd be known as the first prisoners to break through the new system in Loughran House. It'd be our very own escape from Alcatraz.

Before we could do anything, there were a hundred and one things to be sorted out: would we be able to get transport?; would we have to steal a car?; how would we get over the two fences?; how would we get the screw out of the camera room?; how would we distract the other screws? And then, even if we did manage all that, how could we avoid getting rearrested by the guards? Then there was the problem of money, or, more to the point, the lack of it.

I snapped. 'Well, the first thing we have to do is keep this under wraps. It doesn't leave this room, OK?'

Everyone agreed. If it started to be spoken about outside of our tight group, some ratting bastard would tell a screw and we'd be nailed.

It was agreed that me and Cody would be the ones to go. I didn't have a clue as to why he wanted to do a runner but I was glad that I was going to have company. Tommy and John said they'd take care of the distractions on the inside, but once we were over the fence we were on our own. I could feel my stomach jump with excitement.

Tommy took charge of the planning. 'Best night to do this is New Year's Eve.'

I couldn't believe it. 'Are you fucking mad? The *garda* will be all over the place on New Year's night.'

'No, you're wrong. They'll be all geared up for the hassle that usually happens after the pubs close. Between seven-thirty and nine they'll be in the station having a drink.'

'Yes, and it'll take us two and a half hours to get to Dublin . . .'

Tommy interrupted me. 'You can't go to Dublin, for fuck sake. They'll catch you for certain if you go to Dublin. Head to Belfast, sure, we're only two miles from the border.'

I had to admit it made sense. The only problem now was transport, but Tommy had that sussed too.

'You make your way to the border on foot. If you go over the mountains, they'll never detect you.'

Cody jumped in.

'The mountains? Sure, we'll fucking freeze to death up there.'

We all laughed. Good old Cody could always be trusted to break the tension. All that was left now was for us to actually make the break. We would have to get to the other side of the road before the guard arrived. Cody's mother was going to meet us in Belfast and give us the money to get to England.

The morning of New Year's Eve, the four of us sat around the breakfast table for what we all hoped would be the last time. After breakfast, I phoned Michelle and told her that I was going to be seeing her in a day or two. She seemed excited, but just as I was about to hang up I got the feeling she wanted to tell me something. When I asked her if everything was OK, though, she said that everything was fine and she couldn't wait to see me.

I went back to my room and picked up my photo of Michelle. Imagine, in just two days' time I'd be doing all those dirty things we'd talked about on the phone. I couldn't wait to get my hands on that body. Any doubts I'd been having about leaving soon disappeared.

'Get ready, babe, your sugar daddy's on the way, and tonight he's got a real sweet tooth.'

Time seemed to drag, every second felt like an hour. I looked at the clock, it was 4 p.m. Then I tidied my room, made a cup of tea, sang a song, went to the jacks and when I looked at the clock again it was only 4.15 p.m.!

We gave everything we owned to Tommy and John and only kept the clothes we needed for the break. Cody and I decided to take a walk in the clothes we were going to wear for the escape, just to see what it felt like to walk around in so much clothing. I was wearing four pairs of jeans, four tops, four boxer shorts, three pairs of socks, a jacket and a pair of boots. We were chain-smoking as we checked out the fence. Jaysus, it was looking bigger than ever.

Fuck, I thought. If we get caught, we'll get eighteen months.

On our way back to the room, we passed a screw and I swore he looked at us strange. Cody told me to relax, and that I was starting to get paranoid.

When we got back to the room, Tommy had gone around some of the lads we trusted in the prison and made a collection. He handed me seventy pounds. It was nice to know that people were on our side. John fell to the floor of the camera office, choking and holding his throat. One of the lads started shouting to the screw that John was choking.

At the other end of the house, Cody went mad because some scumbag had robbed his CD player. The screws were caught between the two. Cody and I went down the stairs and out the front door. We walked quickly along the visitors' box, through the tennis courts and then took to running like fuck. We got over the first fence easily. Then that fuck of a screw that had seen us earlier came running.

'They're going over the fence.'

I knew I hadn't been paranoid!

We were at the second fence. I gave Cody a leg-up and he got over to the other side. Now it was my turn. I stood back and made a run for the fence. I jumped on the fence, but every time I got a hand to the top the springy wire pushed me back – two, three, four times. I was getting tired.

I took the money out of my pocket and tried to push it through the fence. Sirens were screaming all over the place.

'Take the money, Cody.'

He wouldn't. 'It's the two of us or nothing.'

'Don't be fucking stupid! Take the money and go.'

He tore off his jacket and threw it over the fence. I took off mine and tied it to his, giving myself something to grip onto. When I got to the top of the fence, I untied the jackets and threw them down to Cody. As I did, I slipped and dangled upside down on the top of the fence.

'Get me off this fucking yoke.'

Suddenly I was free. I hit the ground, sending Cody flying. We scrambled to our feet and ran towards the road. We ran across the road towards the fields and Cody fell into a stream . . . the water was freezing, he screamed, but we couldn't stop. We didn't stop until we were two hundred yards away from the road. We stood listening . . . *garda* car sirens . . . fuck! We were almost at the hedging when the searchlights flooded the field. We dropped to our bellies, the grass was wet and freezing.

Lights circling . . . lie still . . . lights off, we're up and running into the hedges as far as we can go . . . Cody curled into a ball, me lying flat. My head was barely covered by leaves, I could see the prison, I was sure we were going to get caught.

Then everything went silent . . . the police were gone! The ground was white with frost, so a *garda* uniform would stand out a mile . . . wouldn't it? No! A voice from behind made us jump.

'Come on out, boys, I can see you. You might as well give yourselves up.'

Fuck!

I looked up and there he was, an inch from my head . . . but the fucker was looking the other way. He couldn't see us at all. I prayed that Cody wouldn't move . . . and he didn't. The guard walked away. We stayed put and started to freeze. Twenty minutes later, Cody whispered, 'I can't feel my feet.'

I turned my head to try to see what was going on and felt hot breath on my face. A bright light flooded the field, stronger than before, and lit up the face that was inches from mine . . . a cow's! And there wasn't just one cow here but a whole herd. Not far from the cows, I could see a line of police searching the field, inch by inch, but they were moving away from the cattle.

I wanted to kiss the brown-eyed beauties. So much for Tommy's theory that there would be no police about! Eventually we decided to crawl on our bellies to the roadside. Twenty yards up the road two *gardas* were stopping cars. We waited and on the count of three, happy that the *garda* were looking the other way, we shot across the road. We didn't stop running until we reached the foot of the mountain. Our hands were frozen and Cody couldn't feel his feet. We could hardly talk because of the cold. I managed a few words.

'C'mon, Cody. We'll keep going till we're out of here. We'll rest when we're halfway up.'

From halfway up the mountain we could see the village of Blacklion. We could also see the *garda* checkpoints. We needed to get to the north fast. We sat smoking, taking stock of our situation. Cody was ringing out his socks, trying to get a bit of warmth back into his feet.

'My feet are tingling.'

'That's a good sign,' I assured him.

Walking along in the pitch dark, we fell into a hole . . . fuck! Luckily for us, no bones were broken. A quarter of a mile from the border we saw eight *garda* on a checkpoint. We stopped and watched them. On the other side of the border, the RUC were also standing guard. It looked like a game of cat and mouse between the two checkpoints, one not wanting to leave before the other.

It would be just our luck to get over the border and get taken by the RUC! However, the RUC eventually gave up and went away. As soon as they left, six of the eight *garda* went too.

I turned to Cody. 'OK, now is our best chance. We'll just walk up real casual and if they try to stop us run like fuck across the border. They can't go onto northern land.'

'What if the RUC decide to turn us in to the *garda*? I've heard that there are some dodgy deals going on between the *garda* and the RUC. And, knowing our luck, the RUC will want someone so they'll give us over in part-exchange.'

I didn't need this negativity. 'Listen, all we have to do is each rip an ID button off his uniform and swallow it. They won't want that getting over the border, so they won't be able to give us up.'

'Not until we've done a shite.'

We walked through the field and jumped over a wall onto the road through the village of Blacklion. The streetlights showed us that the *garda* station was closed, which was a positive. However, the lights were also showing up our clothes, which were filthy and bloody from our journey. We walked along casually and could see the line of the border. The *garda* were standing ten yards from it. We chatted like any two lads would and walked straight past them.

'Jesus, that was some grot you were dancing with tonight.'

'What do you mean? At least I got a woman.'

'That wasn't a woman, that was a human mountain. You could have charged for tours around her.'

I couldn't believe it, we were past the *garda*. They seemed to be more interested in stopping cars and obviously didn't think anyone would try to walk to freedom. We were close to the border now. Behind us I heard a car pull up, a squad car. A *garda* jumped out and called to us.

'Just a minute, lads, a quick word.'

We were gone, sprinting for the line. I could hear one *garda* running after us as the squad car screeched into action. Fuck, he was catching us. I could feel his breath on my shoulder. The border line was getting closer, but so was he. With a final burst of speed, we made it over the line and heard the squad car screeching to a halt – yes! But the *garda* was still running . . .

I wanted to shout, 'Hey, that's illegal!' but I just kept running. Twenty, thirty, forty feet into the north. Cody was a fit little bastard and he kept going. I looked back and the *garda* were standing on the border line looking after us. They seemed to have given up.

I walked along the road. Cody had run ahead of me. He was out of breath but waving like fuck. I glanced around and there was a *garda* running after me, trying to catch me off-guard . . . bastard!

I ran straight for the RUC camera, waving like fuck. I was hoping that the *garda* would be fearing the arrival of the RUC car and that he'd give up. It worked, the *garda* stopped running. He was walking back to the border with his cap in hand. Bang on time, the RUC car came speeding onto the scene. The RUC went straight to the *garda* and talked for a while, then reversed at speed towards us. We didn't move, as there was no point. They were out of the car in a second, wearing their flak jackets with guns at the ready. Through clenched teeth, Cody joked, 'Oh, fuck. It's Rambo.'

All that was going through my mind was, 'How the fuck am I going to bite a button off a peeler's uniform when he's wearing a big thick jacket?'

A small, fat peeler approached us. 'What about ye, lads?'

We nodded a greeting. 'Are ye the two boys that escaped from that wee open prison down south?'

We answered in unison. I say, 'No!', Cody says, 'Yes!'

The peelers looked at each other. 'So which is it, lads . . . yes or no?'

By now, peelers surrounded us. I decided to bite the bullet. 'Yes, that's us.'

From the border line I could see the *garda* craning their necks, trying to catch the drift of what was going on. Things weren't looking good. If I were a betting man, I would have bet on the RUC handing us over.

'So, lads, what are your plans? Have you any idea of the trouble you've caused the *garda*?'

There was something about the way he asked the questions that made me feel he was secretly happy that someone had got one over on the Irish police. I decided to play along. 'We're on our way to England.'

'Yeah? Well, that better be sooner rather than later! 'Cause if you're not out of here in 24 hours, we'll kick your arses across that border quicker than you can say "All Fenians are bastards", OK?'

We nodded.

'So, get the fuck out of here.'

I looked over at the *garda* and couldn't resist giving them the one-fingered salute. The *garda* who had been chasing me shouted, 'Enjoy it while you can, you little bastard! You'll have to come back someday and I'll be waiting!'

We gave them the finger. The fat peeler snapped, 'OK, lads. Don't push it. You're free to go . . . so go.'

As we walked away, he called after us. 'Lads!'

'Fuck,' I thought, 'he's changed his mind.' We turned around.

'Happy New Year!'

I looked at my watch: ten past midnight. We walked into the nearest pub and over two pints of Guinness, we toasted our freedom.

We left the pub at half past three that morning. We fell out of the place singing at the top of our voices as we staggered down the unfamiliar road. I suggested we rob a car and get out of this one-horse town as soon as possible, but Cody said not to be fucking stupid, as the RUC would be watching our every move.

We decided to walk to Enniskillen, hitching a lift as we walked. After what seemed like hours, a car eventually stopped. The driver was a nice fella who gave us a lift all the way into town. I must have thanked him at least twenty times on the journey.

We spent the night at the bus station. I felt like shite. My eyes hurt, my head throbbed, and there was no part of my body that didn't feel battered and bruised. I looked over at Cody and he was in a similar condition. He opened one eye and looked at me.

'Hey?'

'Yeah?'

'I hope she's worth it.'

I smiled, and even that hurt. 'So do I, Cody. So do I.'

Cody's ma had organised for some friend of his to deliver the ferry tickets that would take us from Belfast to Stranraer. She also gave us a few hundred quid for beer, food and buses. Michael Delap, the guy I had been co-accused with, was now living in Manchester. I rang him and he told me he'd look after us when we got to England. Cody didn't want to leave without saying goodbye to his ma. I didn't want to travel all the way to Donegal but Cody had risked everything with me so I didn't feel I could refuse.

Finally, we were on our way. As I sat on the boat, I started to relax. I was lost in thoughts of riding Michelle doggy-style while I held onto her firm tits, when I was interrupted. Cody was having a row with some bloke wearing a Rangers jersey. We were on a boat packed with Rangers fans and Cody had decided to tell this bloke that all Rangers fans were black bastards, to which the Rangers fan replied that we were Fenian bastards! The Rangers fans were debating whether they should make us walk the plank into the sea, when I jumped in. Luckily, I was able to convince them that Cody hadn't been talking about them, he had been talking about the three black lads who had just passed by. They gave us a few clatters and then left us alone.

When we left the boat, we made our way to the bus station. There wouldn't be another bus until the next morning so we lay down and promptly fell asleep. Clearly the drink and the travelling had caught up on us, as we were knackered. The next morning, when we went to buy our bus tickets, we realised that we only had enough money for one ticket.

'Fuck it.'

We decided that Cody should take the bus and I would try to hitch my way to Manchester.

I went outside to suss out the scene. I noticed what looked like a truck stop next to the bus station. I decided to chance my arm and ask for a lift to Manchester. The first guy I approached, a guy from Belfast, said he would be going through Manchester.

I rang Michael to let him know we'd arrived in Great Britain. Then I rang Michelle. She was delighted, and said she had some news for me. I became suspicious. I threw her a few quick-fire questions.

'Are you married?'

'No.'

'Boyfriend?'

'No.'

'Sex change?'

'No!'

'Well, I've nothing to worry about then, have I?'

She laughed and told me not to delay, she couldn't wait to see me.

The guy who gave me the lift said he liked picking up hitchers, as they kept him company on his long runs. I wasn't much company, though, as the minute I got into the warmth of the cab I fell asleep. He woke me when we arrived in Manchester. I looked out the window and all I could see were trees. He told me we were on the outskirts of the city, but if I walked down the lane he pointed towards I would be in the centre of the town in five minutes.

I rang Michael to let him know where I was. As I sat on a bench waiting for him to come and pick me up, an old woman pushed a fiver into my hand.

'Here, son, get yourself something to eat.'

She obviously thought I was a homeless beggar, but I wasn't going to hand it back; I needed a packet of fags.

Michael took me to his sister Jean's house. Later on that night, I got Jean to ring Loughran House and ask for Tommy. The first thing he wanted to know was what Michelle was like.

'I don't know. I haven't seen her yet.'

Strangely enough, I had kinda forgotten about Michelle. The main reason for this was Michael's sister, Jean. She was fucking gorgeous. I filled Tommy in on all that had happened since we'd left Loughran House. Before hanging up, I promised to stay in contact.

I knew that Sandy, Michelle's friend, would be collecting me and bringing me around to Michelle's place. I decided to have a bath. Me and Jean, meanwhile, were getting on like a house on fire, and if Sandy hadn't arrived when she did God knows what would have happened.

Sandy was a good-looking bird. She told me that Michelle had gone down to Wolverhampton, but was so anxious to see me that she wanted me to follow her. I didn't have a problem with that.

Michael told me that he and Jean would be away that

night, as they were heading off somewhere or other. I didn't give a damn. I wasn't planning on leaving Michelle's bed for at least 24 hours!

The journey down to Wolverhampton was a pleasant one, although my mind kept on drifting to what would happen when I finally met Michelle. I was a bit pissed off that Sandy would be there when we met but, fuck it, she'd soon be out of the way.

Michelle's place in Wolverhampton was nice, a little semi. Sandy rang the bell. Michelle shouted, 'I'm coming.'

'Yeah,' I thought, 'you soon will be.'

The door opened and there she was. Blonde hair . . . blue eyes . . . big tits and . . . big belly . . . !

Big belly!! She was pregnant . . . well fucking pregnant! She beamed at me.

'Hi.'

I was speechless, rooted to the spot. I couldn't take my eyes off her stomach. She put her hands on her belly and tried to make a joke of it.

'Surprise!'

My face must have shown that I wasn't quite as jubilant as she obviously imagined I would be.

Sur-fucking-prise, all right, I thought, without saying a word.

Her smile faded. She invited me in. I followed her without saying a word. She closed the door and I heard Sandy shouting.

'Bye!'

I was stuck here whether I liked it or not.

Once we started chatting, I began to realise that she was great . . . but like it or not, she was pregnant, three days overdue. God, this was all I needed. I wanted to ask her how she had forgotten to tell me she was pregnant, but I didn't. I was afraid that if I upset her she'd go into labour, and I certainly didn't fancy having to spend my first night in England sitting in some maternity ward. So I chatted about anything and everything, making sure to avoid any talk of kids or pregnancies.

She really was a beaut, and great craic too. But the fact that she was pregnant meant that we would never be anything other than friends. I wasn't ready to play daddy. My head was melted. All I wanted to do was get the fuck out of here and back to Jean. 'Shite.' I suddenly remembered that Michael and Jean weren't at home. They'd gone away for the night. Reluctantly I resigned myself to spending the night with Michelle.

Michelle suggested that we go to her friend's flat. I didn't mind. After all, my plans had centred around riding all night and now that wasn't going to happen. I told her I didn't have any money for the train but she told me not to worry, I could easily blag my way onto the train. Before we left her house, Michelle handed me a long parcel and asked me to mind it for her. I assumed it was for her friend and stuffed it into my pocket.

When we were on the train I noticed a man with his young daughter sitting across from me. The young girl was at that age where she was bombarding her da with questions about everything she saw.

'What's that?'

'Who's he?'

'Why is a train called a train?'

'How many miles is it to China?'

On and on she went. Blah, blah, blah!

Jaysus, I felt sorry for the poor fucker. She was doing my head in and I didn't even have to answer her. I could only imagine what she was doing to his head! I was starting to relax when the ticket collector came looking for our tickets. I pretended I couldn't find mine, but he wasn't buying it. Then

I let on I'd forgotten my wallet and offered to give him my name and address. He was adamant that if I didn't produce a ticket, I would be turfed off the train.

The little girl was off again.

'Why has the man not got a ticket?'

'Why is the man in trouble?'

'Did somebody steal his wallet?'

A man approached and asked if everything was OK.

I told him to mind his own fucking business . . . big mistake. He was a detective. He asked me to empty my pockets.

'Daddy, why has the man to empty his pockets?'

I emptied my pockets onto the table; there wasn't much, a bit of loose change, a packet of cigarettes, a lighter and Michelle's parcel.

'Daddy, cigarettes are dirty, aren't they?'

'What's this?' the detective asked as he started to open up the parcel.

Michelle started to laugh.

The policeman opened the parcel to reveal a nine-inch black dildo.

Michelle was doubled-up laughing. I could feel my face turning bright red, as I tried to explain that it wasn't mine, I was minding it for a friend. The man sitting across from me was killed trying to avert his daughter's eyes as she asked, 'What's that, Daddy?'

Michelle was still laughing when we got off the train. I was fuming, although I had to admit that if it hadn't been for the dildo I might have been arrested for not paying my train fare. Later on that night, over a few drinks, I did see the funny side.

In the middle of the night, I woke up feeling terrible. I didn't know it at the time, but it turned out that my clothes had been washed in biological washing powder and that I'm allergic to it. I had to get to a hospital.

I wouldn't let Michelle come with me. I mean, what good would she be in her condition? As I walked along the road, I got sicker and sicker and just about made it to the hospital. They pumped me with injections. I don't know what was in them but whatever it was made me hallucinate. I couldn't remember a thing. I didn't know where Michelle lived, or where Michael was. I didn't even know where I was. I was convinced that I was still in Northern Ireland, and couldn't understand why the nurses were talking in English accents. I was seeing dogs that weren't there . . . cats were crawling up the bed . . . it was totally fucking weird.

Next day I started to come round. I remembered Michael's address and signed myself out of the hospital. I decided I wouldn't contact Michelle, as there was no point. She was due her sprog any day now and I really didn't want any part in that. When I reached Michael's house, Jean was the only one in. I was so glad to see her. She laughed as I filled her in on all that had happened since I'd last seen her. She looked at me and there was a sparkle in her eyes.

'I'm glad things didn't work out with you and Michelle.'

I leaned forward and we kissed. It felt good.

Michael and Cody came in and together we watched *In the Name of the Father*, before they got offside and left me and Jean alone together. Over the next few months, things changed.

Michelle had her baby and went back to modelling. I've seen a picture of her in a magazine but I could never feel the same about her. Cody got fed up in Manchester and headed back to Ireland. He was arrested by the *garda* in Donegal. He got caught trying to rob a car and they matched his prints up to his record. Michael got offered a legitimate job in Dublin and decided to take it and start a fresh new life. As luck would have it, he was barely six months into his new life when he got into a stupid fight over a girl. When the police arrested him, they checked their files and he ended up straight back inside. Jean and I stayed together.

We moved to Enniskillen in mid-1997, and then moved on to Omagh, where we had a son called Jamie. Being on the run meant that, no matter how good life got, I was always looking over my shoulder. I had seen everyone else get picked up and I knew that my time would come too.

In 2000, I walked up to the gates of Loughran House. I rang the bell and walked in. It had been four years since I'd escaped and none of the screws recognised me. I guess a lot of faces pass through the gates of Loughran House.

'Who are you here to visit?'

I smiled. 'I'm back to stay.'

The name registered and I was put in a holding cell to wait for the governor.

As I lay in the holding cell, I thought about the last few years: all the planning, all the running, all the madness, all the good times. I knew that Jean would never forgive me for making this decision. She'd believe that I had deserted her, but I hadn't. I hoped that, given time, she would realise that I had got tired of always having to look over my shoulder, never knowing when my time would be up. I thought of Cody, the escape, the chase, Michelle, the boat . . . everything.

The door opened and the governor stood looking at me.

'Well, was it worth it?'

I smiled. 'What do you think?'

Not So Funny Now
– by J.F.

There was one person in our family that you'd never cross . . .
me ma. Oh, Da was a working criminal, handy with his fists
and a right temper, but he faded into insignificance when put
up against our ma. Lucky for me, I was her pet, her little golden
boy, her very own soldier, and there was nothing I wouldn't do
for her.

One Sunday, Ma told me to go and get me da from the
pub, as his dinner was ready. I ran all the way. When I
entered the pub, I spotted him straight away, the soul of
the party holding court over a game of poker.

'Da! Ma wants you for your dinner.'

His cronies all laughed and started jeering him.

'In a minute, son.'

I was adamant. 'Da! Ma said NOW!'

His mates laughed. 'Oh, Gerry, we never knew you were
under the thumb.'

'Better run, Gerry, we don't want the dinner going cold
now, do we?'

He turned to me, dropping a fiver into my hand. 'Run off
home, son, say you couldn't find me.'

I was barely seven but I knew what side me bread was
buttered on. I ran all the way home and straight up to Ma.

I pulled the fiver from me pocket.

'Da told me to have this and tell you that he wasn't there.'

Ma ruffled me hair.

'Did he?'

'Yeah, Ma.'

'And I suppose all his friends laughed.'

'Rolled around the place, Ma.'

I could see she was breathing heavy.

'I want you to take your sisters upstairs and start packing.'

'Are we going on holidays, Ma?'

'Just do it, Jay.'

Ma walked out to the hall and pulled the Hoover from the hall press. The Hoover was where Da hid the takings of any jobs he did. She pulled out the dust bag and money flew everywhere. I took me sisters upstairs and we started packing our cases. It all seemed like a great adventure. We knew Ma wasn't talking to Da over him missing his dinner but they were always falling out with each other. When Ma arrived up the stairs, we were sat on the cases trying to close them. She had a hold-all and it was packed to the gills with tenners.

'Jay, while I'm packing a case for meself I want you to go down to Mrs Buckley's and ask her would she ring a taxi to the airport for us.'

'Ma, you know she won't do it unless there's an emergency. She says that we all take advantage of her good nature and the fact that she's the only one on the road with a phone.'

Ma gave me a pound.

'Give her that and tell her it is an emergency. Tell her me sister in London is dying.'

I knew it was a lie but I also knew Ma was in no humour to be preached at. When I came back, Ma was all packed and ready to go.

At the airport, we checked in and Ma got on the phone to

our local pub. I couldn't hear the conversation on the other end but it was obvious what was happening.

'Can I speak to Gerry Flood, please . . . his wife . . . is he not? Well, when he comes in can you give him a message . . . tell him his wife called and she's at the airport with the kids and the Hoover money.'

Naturally, Da grabbed the phone.

'I thought you weren't there . . . listen, I just called to tell you that your dinner is in the oven . . . no, I won't listen, you baldy fuck, you listen. You think you can make an idiot out of me, think you can have a great laugh with your mates about me, well, see how much you laugh now . . . and I took the money . . . I don't care if it's not all yours . . . you should have thought of that before you tried to make a fool out of me. Listen, I have to go . . . hear that?'

She held the phone away from her ear.

'That's them calling my flight . . . see ya.'

We went to me Auntie Brenda's in England. We only stayed the night with her because Ma knew as sure as morning follows night that Da would be over the next day. That night, Brenda and Ma had tears rolling down their cheeks as Ma recalled what she'd done. Brenda told us there was a house a few doors up going and Ma and us moved in straight off. Sure enough, Da arrived at Brenda's, and we all watched from the safety of our new house as he searched the whole place. We settled into London life very easily. Ma put us into the local school and every day we came home she'd have some new furniture . . . courtesy of the Hoover bag. I liked our new life, everything was very stable.

One morning, we were all sat at the table when I saw a figure at the window. I screamed. Ma turned and there was Da looking in . . . smiling. They ran into each other's arms, kissing and cuddling, each apologising for what they'd done, and each one forgiving the other. It was obvious we were to be one big happy family again . . . until the next time.

Us kids stayed in Brenda's that night, while Ma and Da celebrated getting back together. Next morning, they were at the door with the bags . . . we were heading back to Ireland. Ma gave me aunt's neighbour's sister the keys to her house and wouldn't take a penny for the furnishings. That was Ma . . . that was 1980 . . . but things were all about to change.

By the time I was ten, Da had left Ma for good, and Ma threw herself into her new love . . . drugs. She would go missing for days on end and I'd have to keep the house together. I became a right little homemaker. I'd cook for the girls, do the washing, iron their uniforms, help them with their homework and try to make sure that no one noticed the set-up. We didn't want the social coming around. By the time I got in to school, I was only fit to sleep. I'd awake to the pain of Mister Liver Spot's Gantley's duster as it hit my head. The others would laugh. Mostly it didn't bother me, but sometimes someone would laugh too hard and I'd sort them out in the yard.

'It's not so fucking funny now, is it?'

If we needed clothes, Ma robbed them. I hated going anywhere with her. She'd fill her bags to the brim and tap me on the shoulder.

'Right, son, I'm going to faint now. You know what to do.'

'Ah, Ma, please don't.'

But it'd be too late. She'd fall to the floor with all the grace of an Olympic diver, dragging at least one rack of clothes with her and giving out a roar that made sure the whole store knew what had happened. My job was to start crying.

'Me ma, me ma. She's dead, dead!!!'

Panic would set in. The manager and half the store would be over. A seat would be found and she'd be put on it, fanned and given water. Ma would start telling the staff what had happened, and by the end even I was convinced that the rack had attacked her.

The manager would insist on getting us a taxi home, and us and our bags would be ushered into the car. As we pulled away, Mother lay like the dying swan. Out of sight, she'd spring back to life.

'So did we get everything we wanted?'

I'd just stare out the window, too embarrassed to say a word.

Fast Cars - by Chang

I like driving in my car

It was 1999, April, and we still hadn't seen a sunny day. Everyone was edgy and depressed and I just knew a bit of sunshine would make everybody happy again. Rab was still going on relentlessly about seeing a Ferrari in Galway City. After two weeks' non-stop talk about it, I was losing my reason. We'd gone by the same estate a million times without spotting it and I was seriously beginning to think that Rab was hallucinating.

Rab was a bit annoyed 'cause I was ribbing him about it.

'If yeh don't believe me, then there's no point in us driving around all night.'

'There's always a point, Rab. Yeh don't want to be stuck driving a Nissan Micra all night, do ya?'

Then I saw it. My heart stopped, and a rush of cold blood went from my toes to my head. It was like the rush from ecstasy . . . no, it was a hundred times better! There she was, the most beautiful car I had ever seen. Gleaming, a red Ferrari Testarossa. My little Tessie. It was like all my birthdays had come at once, like Santa had been listening to me after all! Still, being there wasn't enough . . . now I had to have her.

We abandoned the muck Micra around the corner and

bedrooms, still nothing! We'd been in the house for the guts of an hour; I was going to have to admit defeat. We were heading out the door when I saw an old jacket thrown on the floor. Why not, I thought? I picked it up and started searching it. Again, I found loads of bundles of keys but then . . . finally, eureka!

The little Ferrari crest smiled back at me. I kissed it. We headed straight out without a word between us.

The central locking glided open and I sat in the driver's seat. A tingle ran the length of my body and rested in my groin. Fuck, this was almost better than sex. I turned the ignition key and took the handbrake off.

Rab whispered, 'I'll push.'

'Are yeh fucking mad? Sit in the fuck.'

'Chang, yeh can't start it up. The noise'll wake the whole neighbourhood.'

'Even if you were Arnold poxy Schwarzenegger, yeh couldn't push this. Now get in and shut up.'

I slipped her into reverse and she roared. I was sure that Rab was right, that the whole neighbourhood would wake. Out of the garden, I hit what I thought was first, but the bunny hop indicated I'd found third . . . oh, the embarrassment of it . . . bang . . . first and away. Not a flicker from the neighbourhood. Jaysus, they must have been stone deaf or all dead.

Out on the main road, I let out a roar and slapped me face just to check that this wasn't a dream. I told Rab to hit the CD player and, hey presto, as if on cue, Phil Collins started singing 'In the Air Tonight'. Life just couldn't get any better. If I had died at this moment in time, I would have died a happy man. I sang along as we hit the dual carriageway. I put my foot down and, instead of tearing off, Tessie did a 360° turn.

'Oh, so you like to play rough, eh?'

143

This was without doubt the greatest moment of my life. I knew that a Ferrari would be special but I had no idea how special. It was beyond my wildest dreams and, believe me, my dreams were wild!

Slowly, I accelerated to sixty . . .

'I can feel it coming in the air tonight . . .'

Seventy . . . eighty . . .

'I've been waiting for this moment, all my life . . .'

Ninety . . . a ton . . . one-ten . . . one-twenty . . .

'Well, if you told me you were drowning . . .'

One-thirty, come on, bitch . . .

'I would not lend a hand . . .'

One-forty . . . that a girl . . .

'I've seen your face before my friend . . .'

One-fifty . . . one-sixty . . . go on, go on . . .

'It's all been a pack of lies . . .'

One-seventy . . . go on, Tess . .

'And I can feel it coming in the air tonight . . .'

One-eighty . . . you can do it!

'I've been waiting for this moment, all my life . . .'

One-ninety . . . come on babe, only another ten to go . . . come on, Tess, come on . . .

'FOR FUCK SAKE, CHANG, what are yeh doing?'

I came out of my trance just as we ran out of road and headed straight for a roundabout. I slipped her down in gears, foot pumping at the brakes, fighting hard to control her.

The front started heading to the left, the back to the right, towards a ditch. I was talking to myself, telling myself to stay cool. Rab was shitting himself and screaming. I could see my whole life flashing before me and, you know what? – this was the highlight. If I had to go, now was the right moment. The Who were right: 'I hope I die before I get old.'

The car stopped inches from the ditch.

Beads of sweat dripped onto my lips. I decided to stop for a few minutes and compose myself, but I was so excited about my car that I had to tell someone. I rang Jay: 'Guess what?'

He was groggy. 'Wha? Who the fuck is thi . . . Chang! Have you any idea of the bleeding time?'

'Never mind all that, guess what I'm driving . . . right this minute?'

'Chang! For fuck sake . . .'

'Just guess, will ya?'

'I don't know . . . a Mini . . . a Saab . . . a bleeding tank!'

'Be serious.'

'Chang, it's three o' clock!'

'Go way, yeh big girl's blouse.' I reached out of the car and placed the phone under it, putting my foot on the accelerator. 'I'll give you a clue. Well?'

'Fuck, yeh did it, didn't yeh? Yeh got a bleeding Ferrari.'

We laughed and joked, as I described my Tessie in detail. 'But never mind all that. I need somewhere to park it and it has to be safe, 'cause the guards'll be looking everywhere for it.'

I started off again and headed over to pick him up. We drove around for a bit more, me showing off all the moves I could make in Tessie, but then I decided that I needed to get my new car off the streets pronto.

Rab suggested a car park under a block of apartments in town. We drove in but I had a bad feeling about it. Don't ask me why, it was just a gut feeling, but my gut feelings had saved me on a number of occasions so I went with them.

Jay talked about an industrial estate he had spotted, so we headed out there. It was perfect. There was a warehouse full of old wrecks of cars and it was obvious by the state of the place that it wasn't getting used on a regular basis. The lock was a basic ten-a-penny one. Rab headed to the nearest garage and bought an identical lock as we snapped the one on the warehouse with bolt-cutters, moved some old cars out of the way, pushed my Tessie in out of sight and then replaced the other cars. To look in, you'd swear nothing had ever happened here. I dirtied the new lock to make it look used and headed off happy with my night's work.

When I went to sleep that night, I thought of Tessie. 'You've come a long way, Chang, from the first car you ever sat in . . . you've come a long, long way.'

Summer (the first time)
Summer 1988. I was eight years old and bored stiff. All me mates were playing ball on the green in front of our house but I wasn't in the mood, so I sat inside switching channels on the television, looking for something interesting.

I was feeling sorry for myself. I mean, it was always football football football with my friends. Telly was shite, and Ma was cooking another stew. A stew! It was the middle of summer and Ma was still making stews.

Da hated us hanging around the house. He kept walking in and out of the sitting room, grunting at me to get myself out into the sunshine.

'Do you know, in my day, we weren't allowed to sit inside . . . we were thrown out the minute we got up and weren't allowed in until . . . blah blah blah.' I'd heard it a million times before.

'OK, OK,' I said, walking out the front door. 'I'm going.'

I went out into the garden and watched the game. It was boring. I headed down to the corner shop but nothing much was going on there either, so I headed home. As I came into the garden, I noticed that Ma had left the window of her box-shaped Fiat 128 open. I slipped my hand in and opened the door, then sat inside and pretended to drive.

'Vroom, it's Nigel Mansell in first place, he's flying around

the corner, he is the greatest driver ever . . . but hold on . . .
Vroooom . . . who's this? . . . coming up on his inside? . . .
Vroooooom . . . it's incredible, it's the young Irish sensation,
Lee.'

I beeped the horn as I passed him. Beep, beep.

My mates heard the horn and came over.

'Do ya want a push?'

I laughed and said yes. I moved the handbrake off and
started rolling. The kids from all around came to push me.
They were all laughing and shouting and telling me to steer.
I moved the wheel like I was still racing Nigel Mansell.

Vroom, vroom!

The more kids that joined the push, the faster I travelled.
It was amazing. The speed picked up . . . we hit a small
downward slope and suddenly the car was travelling faster
than they could run and I was driving . . .

I was driving . . . I was actually driving!!

I was in control and nothing was going to stop me.
Suddenly I heard a scream.

'The brake, hit the brake!'

I reached down but my foot couldn't reach the pedals. I
looked up, craning my neck to see ahead, and there it was
. . . coming at speed toward me. Bang! I crashed into a
lamppost.

The force smashed me forward and I hit my head off the
steering wheel. It didn't hurt that much but I got such a fright
I started crying. There were screams all around and all the
kids surrounded me, asking questions a mile a minute.

'Are yeh all right?'

'The state of the car.'

'He was bleeding motoring.'

'Ten miles an hour . . .'

'More like twenty . . . or thirty.'

Just as I was beginning to enjoy all the attention, I saw my ma and da coming at speed out of the driveway. I decided it was time to hit the old tears again. I opened the floodgates, as the kids told them what had happened. I could see Da coming towards the car.

Da had a short fuse at the best of times and I knew I had annoyed him earlier, sitting around on a sunny day. He pulled the door open and I leaned away from him.

'I'm sorry, Da, I'mmmm . . .'

He reached in, pulled me close to him and hugged me.

'It's all right, son, it's all OK.'

As we headed back inside, Ma made me promise I would never do anything so stupid again.

'I promise, Ma. I promise.'

All the tired horses

It was 1991, winter. I was half-asleep in bed but didn't want to get up as I was cosy and I knew I'd be freezing if I did. Ed started calling me, pushing at me and whispering.

'Wake up.'

Ed is me brother, me older brother, a fully certified pest.

'Wha'? Leave me alone, will ya?'

'OK, I just thought you might like to come with us and get horses from the knackers' yard. But if you prefer to stay in bed, that's cool too.'

I was up and dressed before he had time to change his mind. I loved horses. I grabbed some bread from the bread-bin for the horses and headed off with him, with the bread in my pocket. Not wanting to wake anyone up, we headed out the back door.

The frost was thick on the ground and there wasn't a car in sight. We headed over the hill and down to Grove Road. I could feel the cold getting into me runners and the sound of our feet on the frost was so crisp and fresh. I looked back across the football field and the only sign of life was the footprints we had left behind. Ahead of us were a load of horses, but Ed is saying we weren't touching them old nags.

'I know where there are better ones.'

We kept walking, and I can honestly say I had never been this far away from home in my eleven years on earth. All around, the city was slowly coming to life.

'Where are we?'

Ed answered as he walked ahead. 'Corduff.'

Corduff was a big estate. We stopped outside the doctor's surgery.

'Ed, there's no horses around here.'

'Wait here.'

'Ed, what are yeh doing?'

He grabs me. 'Just shut up and wait.'

He went into the doctor's garden. There was a lovely black Alfa Romeo in it. He walked up to it, smashed the window and opened the door. He threw his body across the front seat and seemed to be ripping at something. I couldn't believe it. 'Ed! What are yeh doing?'

'Shurrup!'

'But Ed.'

He sat up and ground his teeth at me. 'I'm warning ya, give it a rest.'

I looked around and there, coming towards Ed, was a man in a dark uniform. I said nothing. He grabbed Ed out of the car.

Ed screamed to me. 'Run, run!'

I couldn't understand why. What was happening? And besides, run where? I didn't have a clue how to get home.

The man pointed at me. 'You! Get over here . . . now!'

I walked over. Ed was mumbling that I was a fucking idiot. The man was talking into a radio, asking for a car to the scene, as he had just arrested two people robbing car radios.

I look at Ed. 'Ed, who is he?'

Ed looked at me like I had two heads. 'He's a guard.'

'Is he going to help us get horses?'

The guard kept banging on our front door until our da came down. 'I have two of your boys in the station.'

Da laughed. 'Sorry, officer, you've got the wrong house, my boys are upstairs asleep.'

'Perhaps you'd like to check that,' the guard replied with a smile.

The curses of Da could be heard halfway down the road.

The guards were all huge. They fired questions at us left, right and centre. What age are you? Where do you live? Date of birth? Dad's name? What's he work at? Stand up against that wall till we see how big you are.

I was that small, I didn't even reach the first mark on the chart.

'We'll have to watch you when you do make the mark, eh?'

I've never seen me da looking so disappointed as he did that day.

He just stood there shaking his head, as the guard went on and on. I wanted the guard to keep going all day, as I knew what was in store for me when he got us home.

When Ed was brought into the room, Da slapped him. He went to hit him again but the guard stopped him. 'That's enough.'

Da was spitting his words out. 'You black bastard. What do you think you were doing, bringing yer little brother out robbing with you? ROBBING STEREOS, for fuck sake.'

'I told him we were getting horses.'

He turned to me. 'And as for you, just you wait till we get home.'

Da went berserk on Ed, screaming a million questions as he lashed him with a belt. That night, as we lay in bed, I asked Ed why he'd wanted to rob car stereos anyway. He said he owed someone money.

He lay on his side and went to sleep, and every time he went on his back I could hear him crying out with the pain.

Jackie Chan, eat your heart out

Our local shop was right next door to us. It was dead handy and we were always sent out to get things that Ma forgot: a bottle of milk, cigarettes, butter. I used to stand there looking at the big fridge with all those ice pops. There were so many varieties and each one was more lovely than the next.

I'd open the fridge a slight bit and look around. Sure that no one was looking, I'd push it a bit further open until eventually my hand would sneak in. When I knew the shopkeeper, Martin, wasn't looking, I'd grab an ice cream and stuff it down my trousers. Sometimes, just as I was about to make my escape, Martin would start chatting to me and I'd have to stand there with my balls freezing off. Ah, me poor little willie! Still, once I was outside and eating my ice cream, it was all worthwhile.

Martin was a nice man; he'd grab me and sit me on the counter while he got the messages for me. He'd be chatting away. As soon as his back was turned, I'd lean into the counter and grab a handful of chocolate bars.

Other times, if he didn't turn away, I'd sit there looking sad and starving and he'd feel sorry for me and give me something for free! Martin had a rack with all the latest videos on it. One day, when I came in, he started laughing. He was putting all the videos out and held up a kung fu film.

'Hey, you know what? You look like this guy, Jackie Chang!'

He pronounced 'Chan' with a 'g' on the end of it and, from that day on, he always called me 'Chang'. Pretty soon other people started calling me it too and the name stuck.

Summers were spent taking our bikes down to the Strawberry Beds to go swimming. It was great being in a gang. There were always loads of people around and you could never get bored. The days flew by and every day something happened.

Before we headed down, we had to make sure that we had supplies. Swimming and cycling required a lot of energy. We needed loads of ice creams and bottles of minerals. One of us would go in and buy an ice cream and a bottle of mineral; he'd get a receipt and come out. Then, taking the receipt, one of us would go in and rob the exact same items. That way, even if you got caught, you had the receipt for the goods.

On the way to the Strawberry Beds, we had to go down a massive steep hill. With most of us on BMXs with no brakes, our hearts would be in our mouths, as we only had our runners to slow us down. All we could smell was burning rubber. Ma could never work out how our runners were in such bad condition.

The hill was great going down but the thought of trying to go back up it at the end of the day always loomed heavy on us. We'd leg it along the weir and dive into the Liffey, where we'd swim and mess about for hours. On the way home, we always stopped off at an old man's house to get a drink of water. The old man loved kids and would chat away to us, asking us loads of questions. As he did, one of us would jump over his back wall and rob his orchard. Then it was back up to the newsagent and another robbing spree.

When we weren't down the Strawberry Beds, we were at the canal. The locks made a great outdoor swimming pool when full, but mostly the Corpo locked them so we couldn't fill them up. We'd bring a hacksaw and vice grips with us to overcome that. Once filled, we'd dive in. My mate Decky couldn't swim but he'd still jump in and try to paddle around in the shallow end. Decky fell off the lip and into the deep end. He started flapping around, panicking. I jumped in and swam to him. He was that panicky that he was pushing me under and my face got stuck in the mud. Now it was my turn to panic. I couldn't breathe. With my last breath, I pushed off the bottom and got out. Don't ask me how but I managed to get Decky out too, and the two of us lay on the side spitting dirty water out and swearing we'd never go in again. An hour later, I was back jumping in off the highest point.

Robbing became an everyday occurrence. No day was complete without it. In Superquinn, we'd just walk into the bakery, order cakes and walk straight out . . . no one ever batted an eyelid. In Roselawn, Tuthill's toyshop was our favourite. Tuthill's had everything: the best of copies and rulers for school. We'd always have the best stuff heading back, pity that we never used them. I hated school, and once the excitement of the first few days was over I'd be mitching back down the shops, the stolen copies lying unused in my bag.

Tuthill's also had some great toys, and we'd rob anything we could get our hands on: computer games, rubber boats, remote-control cars, gun caps. There was a library next door with a lift to the first floor. When in the lift, we'd stop it halfway up and pull the doors apart. There in front of us was a ledge, and we would hide everything on it and head straight back down to rob again. Roselawn had twenty shops, which meant that anything from fishing rods, chocolates, T-shirts, golf balls, screwdrivers, even bike lights, ended up on that ledge. Nothing was safe.

I'd head up from my house on my push-bike and lock it with the lock I'd just robbed in the hardware shop the day before. I carried bolt-cutters and snipped the chain off the newest bike I could see. I'd cycle it home, then stroll back up just in time to console the poor fucker whose bike I had robbed.

153

'It's terrible, I'm telling yeh, there's robbing bastards around here.'

And it wasn't just the shopping centre: we'd rob bikes out of the gardens and, if someone chased us, even in a car, we'd cycle into the forest and lose them.

We then moved up from push-bikes to motorbikes and mopeds and granny-chasers. Granny-chasers were little 30cc mopeds with a basket on the front. After stripping it to the bare bike, we'd speed it around the football field until it ran out of petrol. I'd sneak out at night to rob bikes so we would have one for the next day. I'd call for the others but they were never as into the robbing as me. I'd be calling and banging at their windows all night and eventually they'd come out.

One night, I headed to Ingo's and the usual calling and throwing of pebbles took place, with no result. I climbed up the drainpipe and into the window and started digging him to get up. He jumped up and started screaming.

'Help me, help! We're being robbed.'

I realised it was his brother, not him. I had to leg it. I jumped from the window and landed on me arse. I swear, I broke me arse bone . . . if there's such a thing. After that, I decided that it wasn't worth the hassle, so I started getting out and robbing bikes myself, then charging the others for a go.

As we moved on, I got better bikes and became more organised. I even started to sell them back to the people we were robbing them from. It was turning into a nice little earner.

The gospel according to Chang

We started robbing car stereos from the church car park.

I was hanging around with Wardy, whose brother was a brilliant joyrider. I thought he was so cool. He'd be up the Mountview road, which was a big crossroads where all the joyriders went to show off. He was the best by a mile. Every night, there'd be hundreds of kids cheering him on. I decided that I needed to do something for people to start looking up to me too.

We'd tool up with screwdrivers and break the fly windows of cars in the church car park. We'd know that the cars would be parked up for at least forty-five minutes because the priest loved the sound of his own voice. We could be in and out of a car in no time, and there was always someone willing to buy a good quality stereo for twenty-five quid. We'd do six a night. We were rolling in it. The others were into their hash and drink, but I used most of my money to buy pigeons and horses.

Pretty soon every car in the car park had been done, with some poor unfortunates getting done more than once. The priest started saying in his sermons that vandals were robbing the parishioners' cars, and he condemned us to hell. We heard he was doing this, so we stood at the back of the church laughing.

Everyone knew it was us who was robbing but there was nothing anyone could do about us. No one could catch us. The church put one, then two, security guards on the car park but it didn't make a blind bit of difference. We'd simply split the gang in two. One group would make a nuisance of themselves to draw the guards' attention, and while the guards were distracted, the other lot would rob the cars.

No one could stop me. I was invincible, I was Chang.

When the church car park was too dodgy, we'd head to the swimming pool or somewhere else; we didn't care where. At this time, robbing was just par for the course. We'd head in for a swim in the baths and, while in there, rob all around us. If we found a set of keys, we'd give them to the bigger boys, who'd rob the car and drive it around, for everyone's entertainment, that night up at Sheepmoor.

This was known as 'flashing'. This, to me, was as good as life got. As soon as I'd given them the keys, I'd leg it up to Sheepmoor to see them. I was still too young to drive, as I was too small to reach the pedals. If I got back and the car was wrecked, I'd be snapping. After all, I had robbed the thing, and it would have been nice to see it.

We robbed in 'the factors'. This was a factory estate with offices, factories and the council yard. The sweet factories and the ice cream factory were my favourites. We'd watch them loading the vans and, when their backs were turned, we'd grab a box and leg it across the fields back home.

On Sundays, we'd break into the offices looking for money and keys. One time, we got into the council yard and I found all the keys to the big trucks. I was still too small to drive so I gave the keys to the bigger lads and they told me to head home while they took one of the trucks for a spin. I was raging. I mean, there was no way they could get it out of the yard. It was well-secured and the gates were heavy steel. I sat on the fence out of sight to watch them mess around with it in the yard. Next thing, they headed straight for the gate at full speed and suddenly there was no gate, just a blank space.

I was bricking it but excited too. I ran after the truck, laughing as it wiped out everything in its path. Trees, posts, the lights on zebra crossings! The next day, the council workers arrived to tidy the place up . . . in the exact same truck.

It was from the factors that I robbed my first car. It was a Renault, and it was just sitting there around the back of the factories. I smashed the side window and got in, but there was nothing worth robbing so I decided to try hot-wiring it. It was trial and error but eventually I got it going. I had actually started a car. I was high on adrenalin. We had to beat Ingo into driving it. Ingo was the biggest of us all but always scared shitless. He'd start going, 'Chang, please don't make me do it, please, Chang, I'm shitting it, honestly, I'm shitting it.' We should have changed his name to 'Shitting It' 'cause that's all he ever said. Still, we'd drag him over and force him and, once he got behind the wheel, he was grand.

The second car we took off the street, we were getting braver: well, all except Ingo. The car had been robbed before and you could start it with a house key. We'd get Ingo to drive it like a good thing all around the back roads. The guards would find it and bring it back to the guy who owned it but I don't think he cared either way, 'cause he used to park it in the same place and we'd just rob it again.

It was the first car I actually drove. We had it in a field, flashing it, and when Ingo got out I jumped into the driver's seat. I'd had enough of everyone else getting the glory.

I hit first gear but all I could do was drive around in a circle. Some older boys came over and told me to get out to fuck, as I couldn't drive. When they got in the car, they did handbrakes and everyone cheered. As I watched, I was determined that I'd show them.

I headed over to the knackers'. I'd heard that the knackers were letting kids drive cars up and down the road. Two handbrakes for a pound, and they didn't care what age you were. I got a fiver's worth . . . it was fucking brilliant.

That night, I went robbing with two other lads. We took an Opel Ascona, which was the easiest car to rob, and I let one of the other lads, who claimed to be a great driver, drive it back.

It was a cold night and the windscreen was iced up. I told him to go to our estate. As he came into it, though, he went up on the path and hit a tree. I pumped me head, 'Yeh fucking idiot!'

I threw him out and drove the car myself. I threw the car into reverse and then first gear, taking it nice and slow to the football field. I drove it at full speed to the end of the field then hit the handbrake and it spun round perfectly . . . up to the other end and another handbrake.

It was rear-wheel drive so I locked the wheels and put the boot down in second gear. The car done a powerspin . . . around and around . . . it was unbelievable; this was the best feeling on earth. The adrenalin rush was out of this world. I drove around until the clutch went and even then all I wanted to do was go straight out and rob another car.

The next car I robbed, I brought to Sheepmoor. It was time to prove to all them pricks how good I was. Sheepmoor was perfect. There were always crowds hanging around and, with only one entrance, the *garda* could be spotted coming a mile off. Someone would whistle and you'd leg it long before they came along.

People started getting used to us coming with stolen cars and they'd be waiting, screaming us on. An odd time we'd get a whistle and leg it, only for it to be a false alarm. The older lads would do it just to get our car. People thought it was funny, but I thought they just hadn't the bottle to do a job right. I mean, the buzz was the whole thing, not just the driving. You had to be able to rob too. I hated the fact that, when we finished with cars, fellas would burn them out. I thought that was terrible. I know that people would say that it cost more to fix a car we'd driven but that wasn't the point. I just hated seeing things of such beauty ending up in flames.

I stopped falling for the whistles, and even when the coppers came up, I'd give them a chase. One night, one of the older guys tried to stop me by putting an iron bar across the gap. I just drove straight through it, ducking as the bar hit the windscreen. It bounced up and smacked the fucker on the head. Served him right.

Gold medal for Ireland

As I say, Sheepmoor was a great place to flash. Nearby there was a crossroads, and we'd spin the cars in circles around it. I liked putting on a show. I'd come in at full speed, hit a powerspin, and then a reverse powerspin. If this were an Olympic sport, I'd have won gold for Ireland!

Hundreds of people came out to watch. I loved the fact that they'd stand on the path chanting my name: 'Chang! Chang! Chang!'

You'd hear people saying you were an animal of a driver! The best in town!

The king of the road!

The more I heard this, the worse I got.

Then the next day blokes and birds would stop me in the street: 'Hey, Chang, some show you put on for us last night!'

I should have charged the fuckers in! I'd just shrug my shoulders like it was no big thing, but I loved it.

'You going to do it again tonight?'

They'd be pleading and I'd tell them to be there around eleven. Then I'd see the aul ones and they'd start roaring at me. 'Chang, yeh little bastard, yeh kept us up all last night!'

'Wait'll we see your ma!'

I'd laugh and tell them I'd see them tonight.

Sometimes I wouldn't get a car until two or three in the morning. Flying into the estates, I'd wake everyone up. They'd be hanging out of their windows with duvets wrapped around them and a cup of tea in their hand just watching. Some men who hadn't slept in days started throwing bricks and bars, accusing me of robbing their cars. The cheeky fuckers. As if I'd rob the heaps of junk they called cars. I'd turn the car at them and chase them up the pathways.

Again, it was time to move on. I'd rob a car and take it for a nice spin out the country before coming back to put on a show. It was amazing taking a high-speed car onto the Naas dual carriageway and just letting it rip, and then acting like a rally driver on the country roads back to Dublin, to Sheepmoor . . . to my fans!

The dentist's chair

We were cheeky fuckers.

I remember one time in broad daylight robbing a Volvo from outside the dentist's. I was starting it up when he looked out for a moment, but it didn't seem to register with him that someone was in his car. Then he ran to the door just as I pulled out of his driveway. I rolled down the window and waved 'bye bye' before taking off.

About a month later, I woke at three in the morning with an unmerciful toothache.

'Ma, help, me tooth is killing me.'

'Take a tablet.'

'But it's killing me.'

'It's three in the morning.'

'Maaa, it's killing me!'

'Take a bleeding tablet.'

'I did!'

'Well take another.'

'Maaaaa!'

'Go to sleep, I'll take you to the dentist in the morning.'

I got four tablets, watched them sizzle in the glass, gargled and swallowed but it didn't do a thing. I got up and watched telly . . . it was absolute shite. The muck they put on at night didn't bear thinking about: repeats of *Kilroy* and *Sergeant* bleeding *Bilko*.

We were the first in the dentist's next morning. If he'd told me it was going to cost a thousand pounds to get it out, I would have agreed.

I stumbled into the dentist's and the nurse put me into the chair. She was a sexy little thing but I couldn't care less. She could have been a doberman in a skirt, for all I cared. Now that wasn't me, normally I'd have been chatting her up goodo, but I just lay there letting her get me ready.

He walked in. He was busy talking, finding out info off the

nurse and complaining about the traffic. Then he went quiet and asked the nurse to go out of the room. He got me to open my mouth, then started to numb my face. He started talking.

'Nice area this, you know.'

I couldn't answer.

'Yes, great place, apart from the little fuckers robbing the cars.'

I looked up and saw that he was the dentist I'd nicked the car off a few days earlier.

'Cheeky little fucks, even wave to you as they drive away.'

He had my tooth in a grip and was pulling . . . oh, the pain. The fucker hadn't numbed that side of my face at all.

'They forget that what goes around, comes around.'

He pulled, I almost fainted.

'Think that they won't ever meet the reaper.'

He turned the pliers. There was a crunch.

'Think we are all afraid of them.'

He turned it the other way.

'Don't realise that some of us don't have to take that shit.'

He stopped.

'Do you know that if I left you here with this tooth as it is, you'd bleed to death?'

I was shitting myself.

'Oh, yes. You see, I've numbed your body so you can't move. I could go over there, read my magazine or look out at my newly repaired car and within fifteen minutes you'd be dead. Now your mother signed the form so I'd be in the clear, and you know what? I'd say there'd be a load of happy people around here if you did snuff it.'

The sweat piled off me.

'But I won't do that, and do you know why? 'Cause I think you and I understand each other, don't we?'

He pulled the tooth and got me all cleaned up. I legged it; we understood each other, all right.

Leaving school

I got expelled again from school. I don't know for what, but Ma gave up on me and told me that I could stay out of school if I got myself a job. I left but I didn't get a job. Instead I started in FAS (FAS is a government training scheme designed to retrain people in order to get them back into the workplace). On the way to FAS, we'd rob a car for the craic. One day we saw a man fixing the photo machine in Roselawn, and there in his toolbox were his car keys. I got chatting to him about his boring job, acting all interested, and Strach nicked the keys. In the car park I hit the alarm button on his keyring and watched the lights flash on a Ford Courier van. We drove out and as we hit a speed ramp I heard the sound of coins in the back. We drove to Lemming's Stud Farm. Old Lemming had sold it to a builder and it was lying derelict. We drove in and started raiding the boxes in the back. Most of them had fuck all in them but the last one was like winning the lotto. It was so heavy it took the two of us to lift it. We opened it and there in front of us were hundreds of coins . . . pound coins. I picked up a load and started throwing them all over the place, singing Abba's 'Money, Money, Money'.

We enlisted the help of Hugo to count it. Hugo was older and could change it into notes in the bank. We counted four thousand and there was still a load more. I said to Hugo, 'Right, you take the lot to the bank and all we want is the four grand.'

I bought tracksuits and runners, a 125cc bike and a horse named Clid. We amused ourselves for a week on the bike before it clamped up on us, then I turned my attentions back to Clid. He was a young colt, a bit dopey. I brought him to Smithfield to get him shoed. I waited hours to get him done and then I had to walk him home 'cause he wouldn't run in the new shoes.

I decided not to ride him that night and left him in the

garden. Next morning I got up and there was no sign of him. I went out front and there was skid marks all over the place. Kids were telling me that my horse had got knocked down by a car. Both car and horse were carted off. I felt sorry for Clid. I mean, he never got to enjoy his new shoes.

Getting the train

I started to time how long it took me to rob a car. It ranged from nineteen seconds to a minute, depending on what type of car it was. The Lexus was a right whore, but apart from that there was nothing that fazed me.

We started heading to Leixlip to get cars. It was handy, no one knew us there; then, when it got known that we were hitting Leixlip, we just took the next stop on the train and hit Maynooth.

One night I robbed a nice two-litre Sierra. It was terrific, great speed. We stopped it and looked under the bonnet, the engine was a Cosworth . . . we're talking one hundred and fifty miles an hour. With that power I put on the greatest show that was ever seen in Sheepmoor. People were out in their hundreds and cheering, calling my name as I put the car into powerspin after powerspin. To this day, people still talk to me about that night.

One morning we took a Mitsubishi Lancer GLX from the train station. I put the stopwatch on: door three seconds, into car one second, casing three seconds, ignition six seconds, screwdriver in and car started three seconds, and I was gone. Keogh hit the radio and started finding a station we both liked. We were in Kildare, right outside the *garda* station, stuck in traffic. It's the ninth wonder of the world, why there are always traffic jams in Kildare. I mean, when you get through the town there's fuck all wrong.

An unmarked *garda* car passed and one of the guards looked across. I was fourteen years of age and didn't look any older. Keogh looked younger. The guards hit their handbrake and turned. Keogh bricked it.

'We're fucked.'

I drove straight down the middle of the road and took the first turn right. The *garda* were right behind us. Keogh was screaming and panicking.

'Chill, will you? I'll lose them.'

I hit the accelerator and took off. It was a good road. I could see anything coming way in advance. I reached three cars ahead of me, took her down a gear and overtook them on a bend. I could see Keogh grip his seat, and I swear he found religion.

I looked in the rear-view mirror and saw that the *garda* car had bottled the manoeuvre and was caught behind the cars, flashing his lights and beeping his horn. Straight ahead of us was a tractor. There was a small gap between it and the ditch. I knew I would make it. Down two gears onto the ditch but holding it and we were in the clear. I noticed that Keogh had had his door open.

'What's wrong, man, do you not trust me?'

I drove on and started recognising the area.

'Hey, Keogh, I bet when we turn this corner there'll be a load of birds.'

As we hit the corner he couldn't believe it, 'cause there were a load of culchie girls in secondary uniforms sitting on a wall. We got chatting to some of them; they were impressed with our car. We took two for a walk in the field, boasting about the car being our da's. I had my arm around this tidy one when I spotted a *garda* car parking up beside our car.

Before the girls knew what was happening, we were gone, legging it across the field. I knew we needed to get a car quick or get nicked. As luck would have it, we came upon a car with car keys in it.

'Culchies are so trusting.'

The world's greatest drivers

Vinny and I were the greatest pair of car thieves ever.

I knew Vinny was a legend, but in my heart I knew that someday I'd be better. When we worked as a team, we were unbeatable. We had robbed so many cars that I had lost count, yet every night we'd head out looking for something better. Most nights we brought Juicy with us. He was a fat cunt . . . but what a driver!

There were nights when we got nothing. I hated that, hated heading home without having got a decent ride. One night when we were out, Juicy had crashed out in the back of our car and Vinny had a pain in his rocks. He wanted to head home, but I begged him to give it a while longer.

'OK, Chang, one more estate but that's it.'

I reluctantly agreed.

We cruised the estate, our eyes combing every garden, when suddenly I spotted her. At first, I couldn't believe it. Vinny hit the brakes hard when he saw her.

'Chang, do you see what I see?'

'Yeah.'

'Please tell me I'm not seeing things.'

'You're not seeing things.'

The object of our joy was a 1993 Ford Escort RS2000. I was out and across to it with my flathead screwdriver in hand. I checked for an alarm . . . none. Checked the door . . . it was open.

'Thank you, Lord.'

Five seconds later I had the casing off, the steering done and I was driving our new baby away. I drove up behind Vinny and, as a convoy, we headed out of the estate. When we knew it was safe, I pulled up. Juicy was awake and dying to have a go driving. I jumped into the passenger seat and let him have a go . . . I was looking forward to seeing what he could do with it.

Juicy started giving me a running commentary and he insisted that I wear a seatbelt.

'You'll need one, Chang, this thing is an animal.'

We're hitting 120 mph into a bend but the car is sticking to the road no problem. In no time we were back on the mountain road and the crowd were cheering us on. I did some speed flashes, and Vinny did the jump, lifting her three feet off the ground. We were each trying to outdo the other. It was my turn again, so I took off in a puff of smoke, dropped to first gear and handbraked the first corner . . . fucking beautiful! The next trick was a 360° turn followed by a reverse powerspin. Now for my big finale . . . the jump at 120 mph plus. As I hit the rise, the car took off four, five, maybe six feet into the air, but when it landed I still held it firm and made the bend . . . I am king! I decided to do it again . . . like a lap of honour. As I approached, a *garda* car came onto our estate, straight ahead of me. I swerved by them and headed for the back roads; they hadn't a hope in hell of catching me.

Little bag of tricks

It was February 1995. I wouldn't be fifteen until March, but already my reputation was growing. My ma and da were always on at me to get a decent job, but I had a job – I robbed cars. It was great, everywhere I went people knew me. All the fellas wanted to be my mate and all the girls knew my name . . . life didn't get any better than that, did it?

All I needed was my little bag of tricks: a pair of gloves; one cap; a monkey wrench; a vice grips; two flathead screwdrivers; two Philips screwdrivers; one Maglite torch with an extra packet of batteries; one wire-cutters and a small bolt-cutters. Once I had them, there wasn't a car built I couldn't get.

My mate Jay said there was a guy from Navan called

Darby who wanted me to drive for him. The guy was into robbing pubs and shops all over the country. Jay said the money was good so I thought, why not?

Mostly it was as easy as robbing candy from a baby. Few of the pubs had any alarm systems. A simple window job and I was in, opening the fire exit and loading the car with as many cigarettes and bottles as we could get. If the till was full, it was an added bonus. We'd often hit three a night before heading home.

Everything was going like clockwork until one night we drove straight into a roadblock. I out-drove them no problem, but we picked up another squad car. The heap of junk I was driving was beginning to die. We needed to dump it and get new wheels.

With the new car I knew we could outrun anyone. Still, at every crossroads we were picking up more and more chases. I knew by the time we hit Dublin that they'd have the whole place blocked off. I turned down a sideroad and headed north – they'd never expect that. When we saw the blue and red pathways, I knew we were in the north. Up ahead was a checkpoint. We were too close to do a U-turn and I knew that they would have spikes all the way across the road if we tried to drive through. I edged up to the checkpoint only to find out that it was unmanned . . . the peace treaty had kicked in!

Making the papers

Things were getting hot. The police knew me well and I always slept with one eye open, ready for a quick getaway if they raided. I had just turned fifteen.

One morning I heard banging on our door. I peeped out the window but I didn't recognise them as our guards. They're up the stairs and asking me a million questions at once. Where were you on . . . ? Who were you with . . . ? Etc., etc., etc.

'Chang, were you ever down the country?'

'No.'

'Well, come with us because you're going there now.'

I didn't bother protesting, just asked if I could use the loo. When I got into the toilet I saw that my da's runners were there, so I put them on. Outside there were two *garda* standing guard. Our shed was about six feet away from the back of the house; and it was my only chance.

With a deep breath and a huge leap, I was gone.

'Chang, come back, you little bastard.'

Too late. I was jumping back-garden walls like they weren't there. I was like a hurdler, I'd gone over that many walls. I was two estates away and in my mate Cronin's house. He gave me a decent pair of runners and a breakfast.

That evening, the *Evening Herald* newspaper was informing the world that the *garda* were left red-faced today as a fifteen-year-old thug gave them the slip. When the heat died down, I went home. They raided, of course, but I hid in the attic. I got cocky and ventured out in daylight to get a breakfast roll and a Yop . . . big mistake.

I hadn't even got a full mouthful when I spotted the Black Maria. I threw the roll and legged it. I was doing my wall trick when I spotted they were waiting in the lane . . . they weren't letting that happen again. I was in a traveller's back garden. I felt that if anyone would help me, he would. I entered his house and into his attic, hiding under the felt installation. But the bastard ratted me up and I was dragged out and thrown into the Black Maria. Despite the banging of all the kids from our estate on the car, they took me away. I ended up in Trinity House in Lusk.

I lasted two weeks. The lads came down from Dublin and broke me out. I arrived at my welcome home party still in my pyjamas.

I was a fugitive . . . it was fucking great! When eventually they caught up with me, I was sent to Oberstown, next door to Trinity House, but this time I was watched by the fastest officers and only allowed to wear runners in school, otherwise it was flip-flops.

The first chance I got to escape I did. The teacher left the class for some strange reason and as soon as he did I was out the window. He came back in as I descended on the other side but it was too late, I was out of there. I hid in the field beside the school, fully expecting them to chase me . . . but they didn't.

When they caught me again, I was put into Mountjoy while awaiting trial. I loved it, in with all the real criminals. The prison officers gave me a hard time, accusing me of robbing their cars . . . I wouldn't have minded if I had. When I went to court it was full of guards waiting to press charges. I felt sorry for my dad, I think he got a shock with the amount of them. The judge called me a thug and sentenced me to four years in Oberstown prison. Prosecution tried to get my case remanded but the judge was having none of it and ordered that they take me to Oberstown immediately.

When we got there, Oberstown was full and the only choice they had was to release me. The stupid judge – if he had remanded me, I'd have got four years. I arrived home in my father's custody. He was asleep on the sofa. When I woke him, he looked up and screamed, 'You little bastard, Chang, you've escaped again, haven't you?'

It was the second time my case had hit the papers. There was uproar about me getting out. I went on a rampage that night and made the papers the next day. At the time, I thought it was great, I was putting the two fingers up at the world and making the papers . . . I was a celebrity. What I didn't realise was that the guards were getting pissed off and were looking for anything to do me on. One day, on a search, they found nine E tabs on me. I had been minding them for a mate and clean forgot about them being in my pockets. I got a month for each tab.

I didn't mind, there were a lot of mates inside, time passed. But I was just out when I got done for a job down the country. I was sent down for another two years.

Where's Tessie?

It was 1999, April. I decided that I'd hit the gym before going to Tessie. I did a good workout then headed down.

I wanted her ticking over nicely for when I took my girlfriend to the hospital, to have our baby. Imagine the looks of envy we'd get arriving at the Rotunda in Tessie. Nothing but the best for my girl . . . after all, she deserved it. She stood by me no matter what, and that was going to be the most important day in our lives . . . everything had to be perfect. I could imagine her face when she gave me the call to collect her and I arrived up to her house . . . in a Ferrari!

I opened up the shutter and stared . . . at a blank space.

The bastards had found my Tessie.

Life Before Death - by Pedro

Crumlin, 1978

'Up out of that bed now. You'll be late for fucking school.'

I shot up in the bed, the words I hated ringing in my ears.

My name is John: an eight-year-old from Crumlin. Let me introduce you to the rest of my gang. There's Glen who's nine, Anthony who's eleven (the driver and best goer of the five of us), Brian who's ten and only in the gang because Anthony is his big brother, and last but not least is Joey. Joey is eleven and he's the only one of us who doesn't get escorted to school. Joey's da left his ma years ago, and she hasn't stopped drinking since. Still, there's nothing unusual about that, that's life in Crumlin.

That's certainly how things were when we were growing up, anyhow. In a way, we all thought Joey was lucky. Those of us who had das sometimes wished we hadn't, because Da was the one, every morning, to drag you out of bed and kick your arse out to school!

Joey had it easy. He would lie in bed until we called, then he'd jump up fully clothed, wet his hair and he'd be out the door before his ma could say a thing.

It was nine-thirty on a Monday morning and we were in Joey's garden. His ma, who was locked out of her head, was screaming at us, telling us we'd better not bring the pigs to

171

her door. We just laughed; she said the same thing every day.

As we left Joey's garden, Anthony said, 'Are yehs right, lads? Let's head for H.Williams in Tallaght. It's time for our daily buzz.'

Our daily buzz was a big green tin of glue and five plastic bags. We'd hang around outside the shop, waiting for it to get busy. Then as soon as 'Fathead', the security man, moved away from the door, we'd be in. We'd grab anything we could get our hands on in order to get a chase.

The poor fucker. He never had a hope. The minute he left the shop to chase us, Glen would nip back in, grab the glue and leg it. Once we were far enough away, we'd look back and see Fathead leant against the wall, sweating like a pig and trying to catch his breath. I'd say he prayed every morning that the five little cunts from Crumlin were run over by a bus.

He knew us all by name – even called the pigs on occasion, but that didn't bother us. As the pigs were talking to the others, I'd slip in and grab another tin of glue and be waiting at the chipper for the others to join me.

Today was one of those days that he called the police. I watched from the safety of the chipper as the pigs herded the lads into the back of the pig-mobile. Oh fuck – Glen, Anthony, Joey and Brian were done for. The pigs would bring them back to school and the brother would batter the shite out of them.

I needed some glue pronto, this was wrecking me head. I poured some into a plastic bag but kept the rest for the gang . . . they were going to need it more than me. That cunt of a brother had other plans, though, and as soon as he finished beating the shite out of them, he asked the pigs to take them home to their parents. Now the shite would really hit the fan.

Joey's ma and Anthony and Brian's da were certainly handy with their beatings. By the time we met up later that day, the boys all had black eyes and bruised bodies. And poor Glen couldn't even sit down. His da, big man that he was, had leathered the arse off him with his belt.

I felt so sorry for Glen; I hated seeing him in such pain. Of all the guys in the gang, Glen was my best friend, I'd do anything for him.

'What a poxy life this is,' I thought, as I put the bag of glue to my face and inhaled. 'Fuck, man! That was a bad buzz, never again,' I thought as I picked glue off my hair and mouth.

I knew I couldn't go home, not in this state. My da would fucking kill me. So I decided to stay out. I'd sleep in the park and freeze the bollix off myself. Even though I was acting like a big tough man, I really wanted to go home to my own bed.

Glen felt the same. 'That's it, John. No more glue. From now on, it will just be a few cans and a bit of hash.'

'Yeah,' I agreed.

1980

Me, Glen and Joey had got done for robbing a car. We hadn't even got the fucking thing started when the pigs were on us.

Anthony and Brian had been lucky. They'd got offside. I was glad for them – Brian wouldn't have been worth a fuck in the pig shop.

You had to know how to play the game. Once they got you into the pig shop, they'd start laying into you, kicking the shite out of you and playing their good cop/bad cop routine, telling you that one of your mates had given a statement. I never bought into that shit. I'd just sit there smiling, telling them to change the record . . . Bang! Another smack around the head. Good, I knew I was getting to them.

I knew none of the boys would rat me up. We all suffered from collective memory loss in the pig station. 'I don't know what you're talking about, the fucking drink and hash has me brain melted.'

'Well, see how melted your brain is up in court.'

Ma came to court with me. Da didn't. As far as he was concerned, I'd broken my promise not to get into trouble. Some promise! I'd only made it when I was curled up in a fucking ball after he'd kicked the shite out of me. He'd hit me so hard that I'd landed in the dirty clothes basket. My hands were caught and I couldn't move. There was I, Mad Bad John O'Sullivan . . . defenceless! Da didn't half take advantage of my situation, and he clattered the shite out of me for what seemed like hours. That night, as I lay in bed, I swore I'd get my own back. I'd stab the old fucker in his sleep.

That's if Ma didn't get there first.

I was fined two quid. The judge said I was a very bad boy and that I was breaking my mother's heart.

'Now go home. You're to go back to school. Next case!'

That was it. I was free!

Still, I'd made a promise to Ma and I was determined to keep it . . . at least for the time being. That would keep her happy, and it would cool the bad buzz in the house. I was so happy to be free that I even took back the promise I'd made to kill the aul fella in his sleep!

1982 . . . Man, where do the years go? I was twelve years old and I couldn't even remember a quarter of my life. I'd really have to put the drugs buzz behind me . . . nothing but cans from now on.

'No more drugs for me.'

My sister Joanna and her mates started going out with blokes from the 'old county'. That's what we called the middle of Crumlin. We lived at the top of Crumlin – the wildest part, where you're one hundred per cent sure of a fight every night of the week. Our area was so bad that the pigs wouldn't even come in during the day!

Just as it should be.

So the girls were dating. There was Joanna and Lucy, Mags and big fat Babs, the fighter of the group. That girl could pack some punch. Man, I'm telling you. She'd knocked out more blokes than our whole gang put together. Babs was the girl you wanted in your corner when a fight kicked off.

The girls asked us to head down to the old county with them. Me and Glen agreed. After all, we were desperately trying to stay away from the glue and the hash and the magic mushrooms.

One night me and the boys had eaten at least one hundred mushrooms each and, I swear, we got the highest high of all time. The thing with mushrooms was that the more you took, the higher you got. There was no limit to the cloud. Say, for instance, glue was cloud ninety-nine, and hash was cloud one hundred, well, mushrooms were cloud one million and rising. It was scary. Every other drug had its limit but mushrooms just kept on rising. Where it would end, God only knew.

Anyway, like I say, we were happy to get away from all that shite. Besides, there might be a few birds for us to get off with.

We got five cans each and headed down to the old county. When we got there, the girls had drink but the blokes didn't. I nodded to a few of the blokes that I recognised. My sister's fella was called Jules; I'd never seen him before. He was sixteen but I didn't give a fuck. I walked straight up to him and told him that I didn't want him messing her around. Imagine, there's me, twelve years old and barely four foot telling this sixteen-year-old that I'd sort him out!

In Crumlin, everyone knew my gang's reputation and they didn't fuck with us. But these guys were cool, they didn't want trouble. As I opened a can, I asked one of the blokes why none of them were drinking. He just laughed and Jules said, 'Come on. Stroll down to my gaff with me.'

Not wanting to lose face, me and Glen went with him and his mates, Podge and Carroller. They were sixteen too, and I noticed they were at their noses all the time. We soon found out why.

Jules took out three bags: a bag of needles, a bag of brown stuff and a big bag of white stuff. Shit, they were junkies. We'd never even seen gear before and here they were asking us did we want some?

I looked over at Glen and saw real fear in his eyes. I wondered, did he see the same fear in mine? But fuck it. I was Mad Bad John O'Sullivan, and there was no way I could refuse. No way I was going to lose face.

Jules took out a spoon and put some water and a bit from both bags on it. He then put a lighter under the spoon and started heating it up.

The smell nearly made me puke.

I wished to fuck I was back on home ground. At least there I could have walked away and not lost face. But not here, no way. Jules broke the tip off a cigarette and placed it on the spoon, then he sucked the liquid through it into a needle.

'Right, who wants to go first?'

I was in like a shot. I went over to Jules, the nerves were starting to hit. I whispered to him, 'Man, we've never taken gear before.'

He smiled, 'I know.'

He rolled my sleeve right up to my bony shoulder.

'Jaysus, man. There's hardly any fucking skin on you at all.'

He pinched some skin between two fingers and stuck the needle into it. I was half-dreading the needle piercing me skin, I hated needles. But, before I knew it, he was finished with me and was rolling up Glen's sleeve.

'Fuck,' I thought, 'is that it?'

I'd been shitting myself and all for nothing. Nothing was happening, nothing. I'm feeling nothing. I'm looking over at Glen and there's no change in him either . . . except his face and eyes look very clear, not fucked up like they usually do.

I was feeling nothing, not a damn thing . . . suddenly I started retching.

'Shit!' someone shouted. 'The little fucker's going to puke!'

And that's how I spent the rest of the night . . . puking my ring up.

Now, you'd expect that that would have been enough to put me off gear for life. I mean, puking your ring up every twenty minutes is no fun. But the feelings in between the pukes . . . those twenty minutes in between . . . were pure, unadulterated bliss.

I talked the ears off every bird in the place, and they listened! I was only twelve and a load of fifteen-year-old girls were fighting over me . . . they all wanted to be my mot! Now, say what you like, but I knew my popularity with the birds was all thanks to the gear. I wasn't shy, I wasn't taking redners . . . I was Mr Personality.

I was chatting to two bits of skirt that the older fellas had said were gamey, and they were lapping me up. One of them even let me feel her tits . . . inside her top! And the other one, not wanting to be outdone, was forcing my hand up her skirt and onto her pussy. Thank you, Lord! Thank you for introducing gear to my life.

I'd never had that much attention before. I'd never had people hanging on my every word, wanting to hear my war stories. Never getting bored with them. I was twelve years old and me and Glen ruled our world. We had a say in everything, who was in and who could fuck off. Jules, Carroller and Podge were now running for us . . . gutless fucks. They were sixteen and we were telling them what to do!

Then we got a lovely suss. Dicko, an older bloke we knew, wanted us to run his gear up to the flats. There was a lot of heat on the flats but no one was expecting two kids to be carrying. He offered us £100 each, but we said no, we wanted gear. We agreed on 10 per cent. For every hundred bags we sold, we got ten. We could have made forty quid a bag, but we weren't thinking about that . . . we were thinking about getting gear for ourselves. So off we trotted, two schoolboys strolling past the pigs as they searched everyone else . . . nice!

Glen kept look-out. We didn't want to get caught with one hundred bags of gear, especially as ten of them were ours. I had the hundred bags in a cigarette box in my school bag . . . pure genius.

When we reached the flats, we saw the queue of junkies all waiting for the man, the man we were supplying. The first time we met him, he laughed at us. He thought it was mad, two nippers acting as donkeys. Little did he know that the same two nippers were as much addicts as any of the older lads queuing for their fix.

I always made sure to get out of the flats pronto. I didn't want someone seeing me and Glen and putting two and two together. I didn't need someone ratting to the pigs or, worse still . . . to my da.

Although the thought of Da finding out I was on drugs sent shivers down my spine, I'd have to be very unlucky for that to happen, because drugs hadn't really hit yet. The most Da ever did was check our breaths for the smell of drink.

As soon as we collected our 'wages', we'd be off to Jules's gaff. Amazing as it might seem, we still needed him or Carroller or Podge to mix the gear together and shoot us up. It was worth giving them a free bag for this.

Before long, we couldn't get the same buzz we got that first night without having a bag inside us. Not that this was a major problem . . . business in the flats was booming. We were doing a minimum of one run a day . . . sometimes two or three.

We were only six months into our habit when disaster hit. Dicko (living up to his name) got caught with a bag in his house. The stupid fuck! We were only twelve and even we knew that only stupid cunts keep gear in their houses. Now we were really in the shit. Our nice little arrangement with Dicko was gone, but we still had our habits to feed. Our only choice was to start robbing.

Every morning I'd have to drag myself out of bed and go down to the kitchen with a big smile on my face and all chat to Ma, when all the while my body was screaming for its next fix. I was addicted. I'd go to bed sweating like a pig, wide awake, trying to think where we'd go robbing the next day. I hated Jules for ever introducing me to gear. By eight-thirty every morning, Glen and I would be in some office trying to get our hands on cash boxes or hoping to find a purse that had been left in a drawer. If we didn't get money, we needed to get something we could sell. At that time, BMXs were as good as hard cash. A nice five-spoker and you were guaranteed two bags and a packet of cigarettes. We did every school bike shed we could think of.

I didn't realise it at the time but this was the beginning of a downward spiral. Older boys said that once the devil's dandruff got you, you were finished. And they were right, this was my life before death.

1986

It was my sixteenth birthday and, despite the fact that I was up in court on thirty-one charges of house-breaking and one of school-breaking, I was in great form.

Garda Maher hated me; he'd given me so many hidings that I'd lost count. But on this particular day, something was amiss. He pulled me in on a charge of breaking into a school. As usual, I said nothing. I just sat there looking at him, smiling. My silence was usually enough to send him mad, he'd lose it and clatter me around the place and I'd know that I had won because it meant he hadn't anything that could stick. But, like I say, today was different. He'd been in the room for ten minutes now and hadn't hit me once . . . bad suss.

He stood smiling at me. 'I have you this time, O'Sullivan, you little fucker.'

It turned out that Brian, the crier, had fucked up. When we'd done the school we hadn't worn gloves, and the stupid fucker hadn't wiped all the glass. The pigs had found a full print, belonging to me, on a small pane of glass.

Maher wanted me to take the rap for fifty houses in order to get them off his books . . . make him look like the great guy. If I took the rap, he'd only do me on ten and the school. He said it would be a cinch, nothing major, just a few stolen videos. He also said that if I didn't sign the statement, he'd have me for all fifty houses and I'd be sure to spend a long time in St Pat's.

I looked all worried, I even shook a bit. I asked him for a cigarette, he gave me two. I asked if I could trust him, he assured me I could. I smoked the cigarettes as he got his pen and paper ready.

'OK, let's get on with this.'

I looked at him.

'On with what?'

'The school.'

I smiled and stubbed out the cigarette.

'What school?'

Just as he rose to hit me, the door opened and Da stood there.

Maher looked from one to the other. I was laughing. His

face was that red I thought he'd burst a blood vessel.

'I'll have you, boy. You mark my words.'

So, having spent six weeks on remand in Pat's, here I was, on the morning of my sixteenth birthday, standing in front of the judge. Garda Maher was stuttering and stammering because his bluff had been called and he had to withdraw all the charges, all except the school. I laughed all the way back to Pat's.

I didn't care that the judge had given me six months. I was the man, everyone in Pat's thought I was cool. Glen was in Pat's too; he'd been done for robbing a car. We never robbed cars for joyriding; we only robbed them to get down the country so we could rob a pub.

We needed a constant supply of money – our habit was costing us £200 a day each – and there was nothing we wouldn't do to get our hands on that money. If we didn't get the money, we didn't get the gear. And without gear your body would ache all over, especially your arms and legs . . . God, the pain! And the night sweats would keep you awake all night. All you could think of was gear and every second lasted an eternity. You'd feel like you were going to die and the only thing that would save you was a fix. Needing gear never killed anyone, it just left you in limbo, but as soon as you got a bag into you the miracle would happen and you'd be back on earth.

Believe me, I didn't have too many nights like that. There was no way I would let myself go without.

A week into my sentence, my world was turned upside down. Ma and Da came to see me. Ma was crying and looked ten years older than I had remembered her. I thought someone must have died. I was racing through all my relatives, trying to think who it could be, when Ma blurted out, 'Are you on heroin?'

I was shocked. Fuck it. How did they know? I looked over

at one of the screws and I knew immediately that he'd ratted me up.

'No! Ma! Who told you that?'

She glanced at the screw. Fuck him. I told them not to believe that fucking fathead; sure, everyone knew he had it in for me.

I swore on every member of my family's lives that I wasn't on drugs. Eventually they believed me. Now all I wanted to do was to finish the visit and get back to my cell. Some nice gear had come in and I wanted my share.

'Fuck Ma and Da and their stupid whingeing,' I thought.

See, that's what gear does to you. I loved my ma more than I loved anyone else in the world and yet at this moment in time all I wanted was for her to fuck off out of here so I could get back to my little bit of paradise.

By the time Glen got out, I still had two weeks left to do. Neither of us got any time off. You see, in order to get time off, you had to be good boys, and we would never be that. Screws would tell us that they were putting us on report and we were supposed to be scared. We didn't give a fuck. We loved it.

We had learned a lot during our time inside. When I got out, then, myself and Glen went up to see Anthony and we hatched a plan . . . we were going to rob a few banks. We had a contact in England who could supply us with as much gear as we wanted, at wholesale prices. So with the bank money from the bank jobs, we'd head over, buy a load of gear, come home and set up some reliable homies to sell it for us . . . keeping enough back for ourselves while making a good living to boot. Good plan.

About a month after we'd made our plan, we decided that we couldn't wait for Anthony any longer. By now, mine and Glen's habit had risen to £300 a day. So, with Joey as our driver and me with a shotgun in my bag, we headed to Bray, where we robbed a nice car, a Ford RS2000 sports car.

With balaclavas, gloves and two cartridges for the gun, we were ready for action. Nothing could stop us now. We'd made a pact that we'd never go back to prison again, so, if any fucker was stupid enough to get in my way, I'd blow him to Timbuktu.

The bank we decided on was busy, but we were confident and had a fast car. Joey would sit in the car while I watched the floor and Glen went over the counter. On a count of three, we ballied up, got out of the car and entered the bank shouting at people.

'Get fucking down . . . on the floor . . . now . . . or I'll blow your fucking heads off . . . this is a robbery.'

Glen is over the counter and filling the sports bag with handfuls of twenties when the gun goes off . . . shit, did I do that? Everyone is screaming. I'm shouting, telling them to get back on the floor, that the gun had gone off by accident. Thank fuck it was pointed upwards.

Glen is back over the counter and heading for the door. I back out, watching everyone and making sure no one comes after us. Outside, everyone is looking at us . . . the whole street has come to a standstill. I get into the car and shout at Joey, 'Get fucking going.'

He puts his foot to the floor and we're out of there . . . not a pig in sight. Fifteen minutes later, we're sitting in Glen's gaff waiting for Joey to come back from dumping the car.

We were hyper. Things had moved so fast it was like a blur. But there's one thing I'd always remember from it . . . the feeling of power! I had never felt so powerful in all my fucking life . . . it was fucking deadly!

You know what they say about the best-laid plans and all that? Well, it's true, because our well-laid plan backfired. Remember the plan we had to buy wholesale gear in England and set ourselves up as dealers? Well, it didn't happen. We fucked up. We cooked up day and night. All our plans, all our money, all our dreams went straight into our veins.

We made twenty-two grand from that first raid, but two weeks later we were back out pulling balaclavas over our heads again. We were skint and needed money for our next fix. And that's how it was.

Everything took second place to the gear. When we had our gear, we'd sit around talking shite and making plans. And while we were stoned out of our heads, it all seemed to make perfect sense. We'd get started . . . just as soon as we were finished this trip.

Six months later and we were still chasing. I hadn't had a bird in six months, hadn't bought new clothes. I was still robbing cars to get around and the big plan was no nearer than before. But I didn't care. Nothing mattered . . . unless it was going into my vein.

Why are people so jealous? I had found true love and other people hated that. They went on and on about the pains of withdrawals, the sickness, the jail you'd have to do, but that was only because they were jealous . . . they weren't in love. If they just tried the devil's dandruff, they'd fall in love too. They'd see that nothing in this world comes near it.

Every film tries to show you how good it is, there have been songs written to describe it, but no one can ever get you ready for how good heroin makes you feel. All that shite about it being better than a million fucks, better than scoring the winner for your team in the FA Cup . . . it's all ballox. I even heard one person reckon it's like a trip to the moon in your very own spaceship. Well, they're wrong, they're full of shit because, despite all these fancy descriptions, you're still nowhere near the feeling you get from the devil's dandruff. When push comes to shove, you can do without scoring in the FA Cup and all that, you can accept it will never happen, but with the devil's dandruff you have no choice.

Before gear, my life had meant nothing. But the minute I discovered it, all that changed. Every waking hour was spent thinking about how I'd get more, and the scams I thought up . . . wow! I knew if it wasn't for the gear I would never move off the couch, I'd sit there all day watching the telly. You see, gear gave me confidence; it turned me from a stuttering idiot into a big man . . . priceless.

But those jealous cunts in the government had made it illegal. Something that grows organically and is the main crop of some of the poorest countries in the world, people could starve if they hadn't got it . . . and the government go and ban it!

I mean, if the government were using their brains and made it legal they could make a few bob out of it on taxes and keep it under control. Then we wouldn't have to pay huge amounts of money for something that had been cut down at least ten times . . . shite stuff . . . deadly stuff . . . stuff that could possibly kill you.

If the government controlled drugs, there'd never be any shortages. No one has any idea of the pain of doing without. The sweats . . . the sickness . . . the suicidal thoughts, wanting to cut your arms and legs off to release the pain but knowing that you can't 'cause you will need them in a few hours' time when it's bright enough to go robbing again.

We hit the ESB office on Sundrive Road. There was myself, Glen and Joey, but we needed someone to go up to the door and hit the buzzer who would get us in – someone the pigs didn't know. We chose Podge. He had never been inside a pig station in his life. We told him it would be cool – all he had to do was hit the buzzer and, as soon as the door clicked open, make himself scarce. Not that we cared, we didn't give a shite about him once we got our drug money.

I bought a box-type Escort that the young fellas had been joyriding in the night before. It was 9 a.m. and we were in

Joey's waiting for Podge to arrive. I was freaking. The fucker was late and none of us had any gear. The sweats were starting and getting worse by the minute; I was ready to kill the cunt when he eventually came running in at 10 a.m., telling us he was sorry and that he'd slept it out.

We grabbed our ballies and gloves. Joey had a screwdriver to start the car. We headed down to where we parked the car. I collected a replica .38 handgun I'd hidden in the bushes. Everything was going like clockwork.

The adrenalin was pumping and I was chewing Podge up 'cause he had no gloves and his fingerprints were all over the car . . . amateur.

Crumlin was busy, there were people everywhere. We told Podge to walk ahead of us and me and Glen followed. Joey was in the car. Podge hit the buzzer and suddenly we were ready. What looked like a woolly hat two seconds before was now a balaclava. We rushed the door and the thick cunt Podge wouldn't get out of our way, so we had to push him in with us.

I screamed at the two old biddies to take it easy and just get on the floor and everything would be OK. I knew that they were so frightened they probably hadn't heard a word I'd said. They just stood there, looking at the gun. Glen was over the counter and stuffing money into his bag. He'd emptied the cash drawer and was shouting at the birds behind the counter.

'Where's the fucking money?'

'It's on time lock in the safe.'

We swung round to see who had spoken and saw a big thick fuck coming out of the small office at the back. I knew the minute I saw his smug face that he had hit the alarm.

I shouted over at Glen, 'Let's go.'

'Where's the fucking money? I want more money.'

Glen was losing it . . . big time.

'Don't be stupid, man,' I shouted. 'The pigs are on their way . . . come on.'

Eventually he jumped the counter. As I opened the door, I could hear the sirens in the distance. There were crowds standing outside. Joey started reversing the car to get closer to us and people started diving for cover . . . nice one, Joey.

Someone had a hold of Glen – some thick have-a-go fucker. I was screaming and waving the gun around. People copped that it was a replica . . . fuck it, of all the times to have a replica. They were getting brave . . . I needed to act now. I smacked it across the head of the fucker who was holding Glen and suddenly all the brave general public were backing off. As Have-a-go hit the ground, he let go of Glen. But Glen was fuming. He started kicking lumps out of the guy, bouncing his head off the pavement.

'Bastard! Bastard! Bastard!'

I could hear the pig-mobile so I grabbed him and we dived into the back of the car.

'Go . . . fucking go.'

Joey put his foot down and we headed smack bang into a squad car. But, fair dues to Joey, he reacted well. He did a quick reverse and we were out of there. The squad car was right behind us. I was wishing we had Anthony with us now. There wasn't a pig in Ireland who could catch us with him behind the wheel. Joey was doing the best he could but they were right on us. We needed to get to the bendy lanes along the Greenhills road. Once we got there, no one would catch us, but every corner we took there was another cop car waiting to join in. Suddenly I saw a plain-clothes car behind us. Fuck, those bastards carry guns.

Joey was swinging the car across the road, giving them hell, and I was starting to think that maybe we'd make it after all. If we could just get to the Greenhills road . . . then wham! Some dirty cunt of a bus driver decided to make the six o'clock news by parking his bus across the road. Jaysus, what was it with have-a-go heroes today? Joey tried to avoid the bus but we hit the path at a hundred miles an hour and the car was flipping over and over. As soon as it stopped flipping, we were out . . . not a bother on us. No one should have walked away from that car, the state it was in, and yet here we were legging it down the road with the pigs after us. They were fit bastards and, unlike us, their bodies weren't screaming for a fix. I heard a shout and looked back over my shoulder to see Glen getting a baton across the head.

He was down, and three of them were kicking the shite out of him. I was over a wall, then another, then another . . . I jumped at least twenty walls before I fell. Fuck, they'd have me now . . . but nothing, not a thing. I rolled into a hedge beside a shed and tried to squeeze my body under the shed. I was soaked with sweat and I could hear my heart beating. In the distance, I could hear a lot of noise. I could hear the rustling that goes with batons being prodded into bushes. Overhead, I swear, I heard a helicopter, and some woman was demanding ID from the pigs. I prayed to sweet Jesus that if he let me survive I'd never rob again, I'd clean up my act, I'd kick my habit.

Minutes passed, then hours. I started to relax, and the more time that passed, the better my chances were. I would have stayed there all night if I hadn't been so desperate for a fix. My body was aching . . . I needed gear. I was thinking of all the money we'd left in the car . . . fuck. I could do with that now. As dusk fell, I crawled out from my hiding place. I was about to break every promise I'd made to the Lord. I'd have to go to that slimehole 'Billy Boy' and ask him to give me a hit on credit. Oh, the cunt would love that. He'd make me sweat, telling me how he didn't give credit, how he had a reputation to uphold. I'd end up begging, I'd end up paying him fifty quid interest on the gear . . . but I didn't care what I had to do, I needed my fix.

Slam! I hit the ground. Some pig who happened to be passing by spotted me and, before I knew it, I was in the pig-mobile on my way to the station. I snapped, asking them what I was supposed to have done.

'I was just after leaving me ma's and I was out for a walk.'

They laughed and told me that the game was up. They'd been sitting outside my ma's for the last two hours.

The bastards fucked me into a cell and left me to stew. The pigs wouldn't even give me a drop of Phy (a type of methadone). They were trying to tell me that Glen and Joey made statements naming me, but I knew that would never happen. I knew now that they had nothing on me . . .

Suddenly, the sergeant, a big culchie fucker, opened the door and in walked Podge . . . shit, I forgot about him . . . and he was crying like a poxy girl, with snots tripping him up, begging me to just tell them what happened.

'Just tell them and we can go.'

All I could do was sit looking at him . . . the stupid fucker had landed us in it good and proper. When he left the room, I calmed down and started to think about things logically. Fuck them; all they had on me was what that rat Podge had told them. My gloves and bally were still hidden under the shed and I knew there were no fingerprints in the car. In my mind, I retraced all my moves. I knew I was as clean as a whistle. All I had to do was sit tight, and I'd soon know what Podge had had to say. I'd find out when I'd seen the book of evidence.

Like clockwork, a pig appeared at the door, waving my Phy in my face. Inside I was creasing up, but I didn't show it.

'Come on, lad, a couple of lines of a statement and you can have it.'

The only words they were getting from me were 'no' and 'fuck off'. Fucking pigs. I was saving all my words for my thick fuck of a solicitor. One thing was for sure, he would be getting his marching orders, thick prick still hadn't arrived. I'd been on the phone and explained everything to him and he'd told me he'd be here within the hour . . . what fucking hour?!

There was a stink off me that took my breath away. All that beautiful gear was coming out of every pore of my body. I was suffering, but every now and then I'd see the frustration on their faces, and that gave me the strength to keep going. I was on a countdown; they'd either have to charge me or let me go. Either way, I'd get my gear.

I could hear Glen and Joey in the cells next to me, but I didn't call to them 'cause there was a rookie pig outside with a pad and pen just waiting to start writing. He was wasting his time, there was no way any of us were going to say a word. They could promise us the world – low sentences, gear, whatever – and we'd never rat on each other.

Eighteen hours later, we were all in the Bridewell waiting to get called up to court. And surprise, surprise, there's no Podge . . . slimy cunt. Thinking about what I was going to do to him when I got out helped to pass the time. We got charged with robbery, taking a car and letting ourselves be carried in a car without the owner's consent. Joey also got done for having no insurance. We didn't even get a chance at bail.

The screws in St Pat's were pissing themselves as we were brought in. We must have looked a sight: black and blue from our beatings and nearly three days without gear. All I wanted to do was get up on the landing and get some gear. I knew Anthony had got a visit the day before. And, fair dues to him, as soon as we arrived on the landing he had it all cooked up and waiting in his works. I could have kissed the ugly fucker.

The minute the gear hit my bloodstream, all my problems disappeared. No cramps, no sweats and the most beautiful sleep ever. Anthony freaked it, as we devoured all his gear. He hadn't realised that our habit had gotten so big. Still, he needn't have worried, we'd both be getting visits the next day and would see him right.

The high court was packed and we were all giving the same sob story, trying anything to get bail. I looked along the line, trying to work out my odds. I reckoned it was four-to-one, at best. We were giving it 'three bags full, your honour', promising that we'd leave Podge alone and be in our beds by eleven o'clock. And come off the gear . . . blah, blah, blah.

Naturally, the pigs got up and mouthed off about us but then our mas got up crying and telling the judge that we were good boys. And bang . . . we were out on a grand's bail. Ma was great. She always paid our bail 'cause she knew that we wouldn't break it on her. And Podge would be all right, 'cause until after the case was heard, we'd have to keep him sweet.

All I was thinking about next was what I was going to rob. I needed money. No money meant no gear, and that wasn't an option. Poor old Joey would have to wait a few days before his bail was in but we'd look after things for him.

Fuck. It was three o'clock and we still didn't have a fucking car. Twice we had nearly been into one when someone had come along. There was no point going home, as I couldn't ask Ma for money . . . someone was getting robbed, end of story.

Glen was getting ratty. 'Fuck this for a game, let's do the petrol station.'

I looked at him. He snapped, 'We'll do the job then hop into a taxi or the first bus that comes our way, regardless of which way it's going.'

We pulled scarves over our faces and ran in. I got over the counter and screamed at the bird behind it to open the fucking till. We hadn't a thing with us and no one was watching the door, just the two of us freaking it. Whatever, the poor bitch had the till open and we were out of there like a hot snot and, wouldn't you know it, some fucker started to give chase.

'Ah, fuck, no!'

I was knackered. I couldn't do this running lark anymore. I jumped into a bush with Glen after me, and thankfully yer man chasing just ran by. We walked back towards the petrol station and waited for a bus or taxi to come along, praying that the pigs wouldn't get there first.

Luck was with us. We hopped on a bus that was heading to Tallaght and, sitting in the back seat, we counted our takings . . . one hundred and fifty lousy quid. Still, it was enough for a fix or two.

Next morning, we got word that the pigs were at our mas' houses, looking for us for the petrol station job. We were fucked. We'd already decided we weren't going back to court. We'd have to do a robbery quick, as I had to give Ma her bail money back. That had to come before everything . . . even the gear. We'd have to do a building society.

It was going to be tricky, as we had no driver. I would have to go in with Glen, do the robbery, and then get out to the car and drive. Fuck the devil's dandruff, it was really starting to bring us down. Still, on the plus side, we could go mad for a while. We had nothing to lose. We knew, no matter what, that we were going to go down for a few years. We had to stay away from Crumlin, so we stayed with friends in Tallaght and only went back to Crumlin for our gear.

It was back to basics, just me and Glen against the world. The Crumlin pigs were delighted that they had us on the run. To add insult to injury, they had us good and proper on the petrol station's closed-circuit camera. And to make matters worse, we were stuck in Tallaght. Tallaght was a kip.

We hated the cold. It didn't seem to matter what season it

was, Tallaght was always a cold and rainy kip stuck in the middle of nowhere. Grass and prams were all you ever saw; miles of fields and girls barely out of nappies pushing prams. If it wasn't so pathetic, it'd be funny.

Still, it was in Tallaght that I met two people who would change my life: two people who would see beyond my drug addiction and believe in me, and who would never call me a junkie.

The first was 'the Man in Black'. He was a true friend then, and still is. Even in my darkest moments, he never gave up on me. There are scumbags out there that you could end up doing a ten-stretch for and yet, as soon as you were inside, they wouldn't even answer their phone to you, but not the Man in Black. He never once turned his back on me, whether I was on gear or not, and that's saying something for a man who never touched the stuff himself. Everyone knew that most junkies would sell their granny for a bag of gear. Lots of people really let themselves go when the gear takes hold of them. Still, the Man in Black said he had heard good things about me from some heavy people and almost immediately we were doing jobs together.

The second person I hit it off with was the most beautiful girl I had ever seen. She was a vision . . . an apparition. I wanted her so bad, so bad that every time I saw her I got a massive bulge in my trousers. And, of course, like everything that you want in life, she always seemed out of reach.

I'd seen her around Crumlin with an ugly dog I knew. So I asked the dog to put in a good word for me. She came back and told me that I'd been blanked. I lost count of the times I asked and each time it came back the same. Then, one night, I went round to a mate's house in Tallaght and found Dog and 'Sexy Eyes' babysitting. I couldn't take my eyes off her, and I couldn't believe the words coming out of my mouth.

'Will you walk over to my sister's with me?'

What was I like?!

Before she could answer, Ugly Dog butted in. 'She won't, but I will.'

She got up to grab her coat and I thought I had blown it, but Sexy Eyes stood up. 'He wasn't asking you, were you? He was asking me.'

I thought Dog would flatten her but, fair dues, my princess stood her ground. I was in!

As we walked to my sister's, I kept telling myself to stay cool, but inside I was shaking like a leaf. We took the short cut through the fields and I asked her, 'Why the change of heart?'

'What do you mean?'

I told her how many times I'd asked her mate to ask her out for me.

She started laughing. 'She told me you weren't into me, but that you were mad about her.'

The fat ugly dog!

We were halfway across the field. This is when I should have been trying it on, but I'd lost my confidence . . . my gear buzz was gone. Here I was with this beautiful girl, all alone in the middle of a field, her smiling at me with the most beautiful sparkling eyes and the most amazing teeth and I bottled it! She'd made it as clear as day that she was into me and Christ, me, Mr Cool Hand John, the big man, with his three-hundred-a-day habit, was bricking it. I had the girl of my dreams here and I was boring the life out of her.

As I went into my sister's, I asked her to wait outside for me. Inside, I stood watching her and going over everything in my head. I wouldn't have been as nervous doing a fucking robbery. I expected her to get bored and head home but she didn't. So I came out and pretended that I had to go to the shop for my sister's cigarettes. I was trying to buy time, trying to work up the courage to chat her up and get a wear.

As we walked along, she said she'd thought I had stood her up, I'd been so long in my sister's. I confessed that I had half-thought of not coming out. It didn't faze her at all. She said she wouldn't have minded or cared.

Wouldn't care? I had birds fighting over me in Crumlin and she was saying she didn't care. I knew there and then that I loved her.

Eventually I'd used up all my time. We'd crossed the field twice, gone the long way to the Jobber for the cigarettes and back again. We were sitting on the wall outside her house when she turned to me.

'Listen, I have to go in in a minute.'

I gulped. 'Do you mind if I try something?'

Without waiting for an answer, I leaned over and kissed her for all of a millisecond.

She pulled away. 'About fucking time.'

'What?'

'I thought you were totally thick, I mean I dropped enough hints. I've never walked so much in my life.'

We laughed and kissed for two hours. Eventually, after a hundred cancelled exits, she insisted she had to go. I asked her if she was into me.

'Do you know how much I'm into you?' she asked.

'No.'

'I'm so late, my da will ground me for two weeks. That's how much I'm into you.'

She was gone, leaving me the happiest man in Tallaght. Unfortunately, her father did ground her, and the only way I could make contact with her was through the notes I gave to her friends.

And that was it. They were the only two good things to come out of Tallaght for me. I came across some scumbags and low lifes, fellas who would rob their own mother, but just for those two people all my time in Tallaght was worth it.

There were others I would meet and work with, other good blokes from Tallaght: real friends, like the latest crew-member, J.P., the Pizzaman. J.P. loved his knives and had a new baby, a Mac 10 sub-machine gun. He was mad into pizza, especially Gino Ginelli specials. He was a young drug-pusher, but a good friend, and with the right crew he could start making some serious money for himself. Before long, we were that right crew.

J.P. had two cars parked offside. One was a Cavalier 18i and the other a VW Golf GTI. Not that good for tonight's work. The Golf was great for bank jobs but tonight we needed bodies and space for cigarettes. We had sussed two small garages face to face just outside Naas. They would be a piece of cake.

When we got to Tallaght, there was a queue of fellas wanting to join our crew. We already had five so we only needed one more. I told them to fight for the place, and without thinking headed into the Man in Black's gaff. When we came out, they were all knocking lumps out of each other. I grabbed the first fella I saw who was still standing and we drove off, leaving the others still fighting.

When I worked with the old crew in Crumlin, we used to share everything. If a fella didn't make the job, he still got his cut. In Tallaght, it was dog eat dog. We didn't trust anyone, and, even though our crew were solid, me and Glen never told them where we were going until we got there.

The two garages in Naas were a doddle to get into, and the trucks parked in the forecourt prevented anyone from seeing a thing. We were out of there in minutes. We got 750 boxes of 200-pack cigarettes. We had a buyer in Crumlin all ready to take the lot at a tenner a go, no messing about with splits and all that shit. OK, we'd get more selling them separately but it was too much like hard work. Besides, the four hundred pounds cash we'd nabbed would keep us going for the hour or two it would take to get the cash for the ciggies. We even robbed two poor boxes. It sounds terrible, I know, but they were full to the brim. And you know the old saying, 'Charity begins at home'.

With the boxes stacked at the door, I strolled out onto the road and started walking towards Dublin. That was the signal that we were finished and ready to go. When the Man in Black and J.P. saw me, they flashed their lights and I walked back to the garage. As I approached, I started pissing myself laughing, for there was Glen stuffing himself with chocolate. He was like a big kid. He had a big fucking bag and was stuffing it full of Mars bars and any other chocolate he could find.

We were all having great craic, but we knew as soon as we hit the road we'd have to snap out of it. Robbing down the country is easy, it's avoiding the roadblocks and car chases on the way back that's difficult.

Finally, we were on our way. The Man in Black was driving our car. He was a great driver and things were going so so smooth. Then, up ahead, we spotted the others. They were flashing us, so we were thinking, 'Fuck, there must be a roadblock ahead.'

But no, they had a flat. We dragged everything out of the boot looking for the spare tyre, and wouldn't you know it . . . there was none. We cursed the owner from a height. People like him should be fucking shot, irresponsible cunt!

We had a major dilemma on our hands. If the GTI was to take all the cigarettes home, we'd have to make at least three trips. And there was no way that the pigs wouldn't have come by in that time and noticed something fishy. We decided to hide all the cigarettes in a field. Johnny would drive his car up the road a few miles and park it up. Fuck, it would wreck the wheel driving on a flat, but we didn't care. We'd follow him, collect him and then come back tomorrow in a van and get the cigarettes.

So we were driving along, messing around and buzzing off each other, when we came into Saggart, and as we rounded the bend there it was . . . a roadblock!

The Man in Black just hit the handbrake and we span around and were heading the way we came . . . at speed. We were the only car on the road and we knew the chase was on. I loved a good chase . . . especially when you had a good driver and a fast car under your arse. The Man in Black left the pig-mobile for dust and we were all happy again. We were heading to Newlands Cross when disaster hit again . . . there were four squad cars blocking the road. The Man in Black performed a spin and we were heading back toward Naas . . . on the wrong side of the dual carriageway. We were knocking wing mirrors off cars as they swerved to avoid us. The Man in Black was cool. He was hitting the accelerator, and we were at eighty miles an hour and rising.

The pigs had radioed ahead and the Saggart pig-mobile was coming straight at us. The Man in Black played chicken and the police bottled it. Brilliant! We were free, and my adrenalin was pumping like mad.

We were plain sailing again. I knew if we took the Saggart road this time, there would be no one in our way. And once we got to Tallaght, the Man in Black would lose them easily. Up ahead, cars were stopped, but even if it was a roadblock we could turn off into one of the many laneways.

Suddenly we spotted a 2.8 GL detective (dick) car. It was fast, but too big for these roads, with their tight bends. Still, we couldn't work out what the dicks were doing here. This was just a regular car chase and the dicks were never out for them. Sure, on any given night there were about twenty chases in Tallaght alone.

The Man in Black suddenly shouted, 'Ah, fuck this for a game of soldiers!'

He headed for the Fortunestown road. That road was as

windy as fuck, and the pigs always bottled it and slowed down. Once again, there were no lights behind us. We were almost out the other end and, fucking hell, we saw they'd a van and two cars blocking the road.

'Jesus Christ!' I shouted. 'What's with all the pigs tonight?'

Before anyone could answer, the Man in Black told us all to hold tight and he rammed right into them. They scattered: pigs jumping for cover, roaring and shouting. There was glass everywhere, and a few brave pigs smashed our side windows with battens and bricks.

Still, the Man in Black had gotten us through the block. The car was fucked, a flat tyre and hardly any glass in the windows, but who cared, we'd dump it as soon as we could.

Christ Almighty! Around the bend there were more pigs in vans and cars. The Man in Black had his foot to the floor but the car was giving nothing. We all knew the score, it was every man for himself now. He'd ram the pigs, and in the confusion we'd leg it. We were all getting ready to jump when a squad car rammed us, pinning us against a wall. None of us could even move.

I had never seen so many police on a chase in my life, not even for a bank robbery. As they pulled us out of the car, they started beating us. I could hear people shouting at them to stop, that they were going to kill us, but they didn't seem to care. Eventually they threw us all into separate squad cars and brought us to Tallaght Station.

We got the worst beating ever that night. Every station we came across had their fattest pigs ready to give us a bit of payback.

I got knocked out. I don't know how long I was out for but cold water was bringing me around. And amid all my pain, my drug buzz was calling, bringing its own kind of torment . . . I blanked out again.

This time I was woken by the worst smell in the world . . .

Smelly Breath Kelly. The bastard must have eaten nothing but garlic and onion before coming in to interview you. He dragged me up and pushed his face into mine. He was laughing, saying that he had me and Glen.

Many's the time he had handcuffed me and dragged my head back, holding his face an inch away from mine. I swear, you just felt like puking with the smell of the cunt.

'Right, John,' says he. 'Before you even start your "I know nothing" shite I'll tell you what I know, will I? All your new Tallaght mates have made statements . . .'

'Yeah, right, Kelly.'

He was smiling like a Cheshire cat. 'The six of you went off in two cars. A GTI and a Cavalier. You wouldn't let any of the other lads go because you wouldn't have had room for them with all the cigarettes. Do I need to go on?'

'I've nothing to say. I want my solicitor and a doctor.'

He was fuming. 'I'll give you one more chance, John. I have you and Glen for a seven-stretch as it is. We have your faces as clear as day on the petrol station CCTV and there's also the building society. So do yourselves a favour . . . a few lines of a statement and we'll go easy on you . . . you have my word.'

It was like a game of tennis. He'd come with his offer, I'd knock him back and ask for my solicitor. As it went on, he started to lose it, and that was all I needed to see. 'Cause if he'd got statements from the others, he wouldn't have been working so hard on me. It was proof that not one of the crew we took with us that night had ratted. They were all stand-up blokes and I still trust each one of them one hundred per cent.

From a boy to a man – 1988

Still, I ended up doing eight years. I was only seventeen, but I was sent to Mountjoy, as the junior prisons were full. The Joy or Rob Jules, as it's known in Dublin slang, was like being back in the flats with the amount of gear there was.

I remember my first day. I made a right prick of myself. I should have stayed in Pat's until I was twenty-one but I was acting the bollix, fucking with the screws' heads by telling them their sisters and wives were great rides. I'd do all the actions as though I was doing them doggy-style, slapping their arses and them screaming, 'Fuck me harder, John, fuck me hard, big boy.'

It was great to see them snap. OK, I'd end up black and blue from the beating, but it was worth every dig. Because of this, they sent me to the men's prison. I was really looking forward to it. I'd heard all the stories of what happened on the wings. Every day screws were getting kicked senseless and I wanted to be a part of that.

Pat's was always trying to get you back into school, as if you were some kind of a kid. Other prisons were the same, but none of that shite went on in the Joy. The only learning I was looking forward to was mixing with bank robbers and drug barons and picking up a few tips for when I got out.

On my first day in the Joy, a screw was shouting, 'Get your kit, NOW, O'Sullivan.'

He shouted it again before I reacted. I was busy looking at two dead cockroaches. At least, I hoped they were dead because they were fucking huge. I'd heard that the roaches were that big in the Joy that you could ride one bareback across the landing and, looking at the size of these two, I was beginning to think that maybe it was true.

I got my kit and followed the screw up the stairs. He was taking me to A Wing. Halfway along the landing, he stopped at a door and opened it to reveal the dirtiest cell I'd ever seen. As soon as I entered, the cell door slammed behind me. The cells here were all the same size as the ones in Pat's, but the only furniture in this one was a chair.

'What the fuck?'

In Pat's we had a chair and a table, a bed, a little locker and a piss pot. We even had a washbasin to wash in. But this cell was disgusting, with toothpaste and shite all over the walls. Reality kicked in and my smile was gone . . . fuck! No one told me about this! I want to be back in Pat's!

But I was here now, and I needed to get to grips with things. In a few weeks I would get all my possessions, but for now it was important to get a smile back on my face, it was important not to let them see a single weakness.

First things first. I had to get water and clean this place up, the last guy must have been a right dirt-bird. I could hear the screws outside. Lunchtime must have been over. I'd get to see Glen soon. My door opened and a screw asked my name.

'Fuck off! Never mind my name, get me a fucking bed . . . now!'

He just stood there laughing . . . the fucker's laughing.

'What's so fucking funny?'

He could hardly talk, he was laughing so much. I was starting to lose it.

'Get your kit, son, you're going to A3 . . . this is just a holding cell.'

I walked out like I knew all along that it was a holding cell, but I'm feeling like a sad cunt. I hadn't even pulled the chair off the wall.

As we walked along the landing, I could hear familiar voices: Harry, Horse, Anthony, Glen and the Man in Black. Everyone was asking after me, but Glen and the Man in Black told them all to fuck off, that John didn't have any gear. I was just about to tell them that I had some – 'cause I had two Gs – when the Man in Black whispered to me to say nothing until we were offside.

There were fellas coming up to me and giving me bear hugs as though they were long-lost relatives, but I didn't know them from Adam.

My new cell contained all the things I was used to in Pat's, and the landing was full of faces I knew from Crumlin or Pat's. There were three crews on A3: Ballyer, Coolock and our Crumlin one. We all got on well together and backed each other up . . . The year was 1988 and I was on top of the world!

In the cell, I split my gear with Glen and a few Crumlin heads that he and the Man in Black had OK'd. The Man in Black got a prison twenty bag. Not that he'd ever touch the gear, but he'd swap it for a nice bit of hash on the landing. Some pricks kept knocking on my door, trying to make out that they were mates and that if I looked after them they'd see me right on their next visit. It was a load of bollix, but I'd keep them sweet with the same line, 'I've to look after me mates first. You know that if I gave you gear first, they'd rip your fucking neck off. But if there's anything left over, you'll be first to hear.'

You had to talk shite, keeping everyone happy was important. Prison teaches you that. It's survival of the fittest, and you'd promise the sun, moon and stars to someone who had gear. And I suppose, at the time, you'd mean it too, but once you got the gear that all changed . . . fuck everyone else except yourself.

I suppose I should have felt sorry for the poor cunts. I mean, I knew what it was like going to your cell at seven-thirty and not having a bit of shit to get you through the night: feeling the sweats coming on . . . feeling every ache of bone and muscle, feeling like death but knowing you're going to live because dying is too easy; swearing to every god and on every relative's grave that you'll never touch the stuff again if they just stop the pain. And right up to the minute that you got your next fix, you'd mean it. Then it was off to heaven again, waffling the ears off some poor cunt, feeling on top of the world . . . feeling untouchable.

I was lucky; I always had my own works. I used some citric acid to break up the gear and cooked it on my spoon. I added a cigarette filter and then sucked it up with my needle. Now the hard bit . . . finding a vein; they were all fucked. Although I wasn't as bad as some that I knew. I was just about to score when the door burst open and a screw was standing there . . . fuck, I'm done!

He was shouting. 'You lot, get the fuck off my landing and out into the yard!'

I slid my works up my sleeve, hoping he hadn't seen me and praying I could get past him and out to the yard.

Suddenly, I realised that the Joy isn't like Pat's. Johnny, Ed and Foxy pinned the screw to the wall. Ed had him by the neck so he couldn't shout. He whispered into his ear, 'Listen, you're new so you don't know the rules . . . our rules. So I am going to tell you. This is our landing, understand? We leave the landing when we want, do what we want, and if you see something you don't like . . . turn away . . . got it? Now if you do that for us, we'll make you look good in front of the governor, OK?'

The screw's face was white but we could tell by his eyes that he knew the suss. He tried to save face. 'Listen, you, just keep that shit out of sight.'

He was ours. He was off down the landing like the good little ant that he was. We called the screws ants 'cause that's what they reminded us of when the alarm was hit. They'd come flying down the landing like a little army of worker ants. Still, I wasn't taking any chances. I shot up the minute the door closed.

The Joy was the coolest place on earth. I was seventeen and dying to make a name for myself. I was on a landing with my mates, hanging with the big boys and getting visits from my princess . . .

What more could a body need?!

Never Enough – by Mark Key

There was a time when I thought I could never have enough money, and that I'd never tire of my luxurious lifestyle. I thought I was entitled to cruise down easy street and enjoy wild parties, fast cars and even faster women!

It wasn't hard to achieve my lifestyle, once you knew how high the stakes were and how low you'd have to stoop to get there. Dignity and self-respect had to go out the window . . . along with your freedom.

It had all seemed so different when I was on the outside looking in. I was like a kid standing outside a sweetshop, licking my lips as I ogled all the mouth-watering goodies on display in the window. I would wish my life away, as I longed to get into that shop and binge to my heart's delight! I never stopped to think that maybe the sweets I lusted after might not taste as nice as they looked.

Once I stepped into my fast lifestyle, there was no going back. I was swept away on the crest of a wave; my feet barely touched the ground. I was Mr Popular. Suddenly people I hardly knew were my 'best friends', I was invited to all the best parties and women hung on my every word. I was untouchable, bullet-proof, invincible! And all because I was carrying wads of cash and bags of the white lady.

My phone rang night and day with people issuing

invitations to parties . . . asking me if I wanted to 'hang out'. But I wasn't a fool. I knew it wasn't my sparkling personality they were after, it was the little bag I had in my pocket that interested them.

Most of the time this didn't bother me, but sometimes I got really pissed off. Now, don't get me wrong, I'm no angel. And I'll admit that I've done some bad things in my time, things I'm not proud of, but at least I was never two-faced.

Despite my fast car, ready cash and bags of coke, I had no friends. So when my phone rang, I was only too eager to accept the invite that was being offered . . . and I must admit, I got a certain amount of enjoyment watching these no-hopers falling over themselves in a bid to be my best friend.

I didn't realise it at the time, but I was standing on the edge of a very slippery slope. I fooled myself into believing that I was having the time of my life. I bought drinks for my new 'friends' and I was forever lending money to people I knew would never pay it back.

When at first you start riding the wave, you really enjoy it, you love it. And the fact that your wave is higher than anyone else's, and that everyone wants to be on your wave, leads you to believe you're invincible. But what you tend to forget is that every wave, no matter how powerful, ends up back on the beach . . . and when my wave hit the beach, I fell off in spectacular fashion.

I ended up all alone in a hotel room with a bed covered in cash, a bag of coke in my lap and a gun pointed at my head. I wanted to blow my brains out . . . I wanted to go out in style.

But I didn't get the chance to go anywhere; I got arrested and ended up in the pad. After spending a week in the pad, I still wanted to end it all. I couldn't see any light at the end of the tunnel and I couldn't face another stretch in prison.

The minute they put me into a regular cell, I started to

think about strangling myself. But before I could formulate a plan, fate stepped in.

I was collecting my clothes when I overheard two officers talking. They were talking about a rapist who was being moved onto my landing. According to them, the protection landing was full and they had nowhere else to put him. Normally, hearing something like that would send me wild, but I had too much on my mind to be worrying about some hairy.

I was locked into my cell. I took my medication and went out for the count. I don't know for how long I was asleep but I woke to the sound of a screwess screaming. I jumped up. For some strange reason, I thought that the rapist had exposed himself to her.

I started banging my door.

'Miss, is that dirty rapist causing you problems?'

'Yes.'

I began to shout at the rapist, telling him that if he didn't give it a rest I would kill him. I shouted at the top of my voice, and when the other prisoners asked what was up, I told them and they started shouting too.

The shouting went on for ages.

Eventually it quietened down and the screwess came to my door.

'Thanks for that.'

'No problem, no one deserves that.'

She smiled. 'Not even a screwess, eh?'

We both laughed. She gave me a cigarette and, as I lit it, she handed me a brown envelope. I lay back on my bed and opened it. It contained two things. One was a letter from a girl I had met at one of the many parties I had attended; she'd heard I was in prison and thought I could do with a friend.

The second was a handmade fathers' day card from my

daughter. I can't explain it but that brown envelope was the turning point for me. No amount of money could buy me the feeling I got when I read my little girl's card. And I realised that, after all my striving for the good things in life, the things that are priceless cost nothing.

When my children visit me now, I look into their eyes and I get a high: a high I could never get from drugs. OK, so I'm in jail, but jail's not forever.

I used to think I needed money, that I could never have enough money no matter how much I had and that I was nothing without it . . . and now I couldn't care about it less.

Appendix –
It's Christmas, Carol

It's Christmas, Carol was how the concept for this book began. We had just had a huge success in the Midlands Prison with our first play, *Sex, Lies and Butterflies*. The inmates in our writing group were all excited about drama and so I decided that we should try writing something together and put it on as a Christmas show. When I asked the group what they wanted to write about, they replied, collectively, 'drugs'. I didn't want us to write the typical drug story – where the author blames everyone but himself for his addiction – and wanted it to be a moral tale. I worked on the main backbone of the story and got the lads to act it out and bring the narrative to life with their own lingo.

I had just heard a beautiful Tom Waits song called 'Rainbow Sleeves', which I felt told the story of a mother's love for her son, even though he had fallen on hard times with drink. I felt that that would ring a familiar bell with the lads, as often it is only their mothers that stand by them. As a rule, I never allowed pen or paper into my drama workshops. The format was always the same: we worked together as a group, I wrote it up and then we re-enacted it to see if it worked and what had to be changed, etc. The reason for this format was that even people with weak reading and writing skills could still feel a real part of the group.

The play ran for three days and played to all four wings of the Midlands Prison. The lads loved it, and indeed quite a few of the players gained nicknames that still stick with them today. Many of those involved in the play subsequently felt ready to start writing off their own steam, and six of the stories in this book are written by members of that group. Apart from the mother in the play, who was played by Cabrini Cahill, all of the roles were acted by prisoners.

It's Christmas, Carol

The Characters
In order of appearance:

PETER KELLY: A hard-drinking man (47).

CAROL KELLY: Peter's wife (45). Long-suffering woman, afraid of her bully husband.

LUKE KELLY: Peter and Carol's younger son (22). A hopeless junkie.

JOHN: Friend of Luke's from way back (22).

TOWNY: Robber and junkie (24).

DRUG-DEALER: Well-dressed, respectable-looking dealer (28).

HIPPO: Minder. Big but thick (34).

SAM KELLY: Peter and Carol's older son (24). A hard-drinker, like his father.

MAN: Ordinary American (30).

RICH MAN: Big fur coat with cigar, arrogant (50).

MR BLOOMINGDALE: Well-dressed and bad-tempered (60).

SANTA 2: Ordinary American (40).

PAULY: Cheery youngster (18).

TOMMO: Wannabe leader (19).

NUGGET: Foolish (19).

JIMMY: Hard man (19).

O'HOGAN: Prison officer (45).
YOUTH: A hopeless junkie (18).

INTERNAL. KELLY SITTING ROOM. DAY.

> [*A small, sparsely furnished kitchen-cum-sitting room in a working-class area of Dublin.* CAROL *is putting decorations on the Christmas tree. She is humming along as Christmas music plays.* PETER *walks in and takes off his coat.*]

PETER: Hello, pet, I'm telling yeh, it's brass monkeys out there.

CAROL: Really?

PETER: [*Sits.*] Ah, don't be like that.

CAROL: Like what?

PETER: I only had a couple of pints with the lads, yeh know, seeing how we were breaking up for the Christmas.

CAROL: I never said a thing.

PETER: [*Sighs.*] Do they teach that at girls' schools? The ability to let men know you're peeved with them without ever saying a thing. I swear, I had three pints . . . that's all. Three lousy pints and I get all this . . . the silent treatment. It's Christmas, Carol, for fuck sake.

CAROL: I didn't say a thing, but yeh could have told me you were going for a drink. I wouldn't have made dinner if I'd known you were going to be so late.

PETER: I knew you'd be annoyed. I said it to the lads.

CAROL: All you had to do was ring. That's what you got the mobile phone for.

PETER: Ah, where is the fucking dinner and I'll eat it? Jaysus, anything to stop yeh moaning.

CAROL: It's in the bin. [*She feels his eyes burn into her, and turns to face him.*] It was freezing.

PETER: What did we get a microwave for?

211

[PETER *stands and walks around impatiently, then goes to the press and takes out a bottle of whiskey and a glass. He takes them back to the table and pours. She has watched the whole process. Just as he is about to put the glass to his lips, he turns to face her.*]

PETER: It's Christmas, Carol!

CAROL [*turning back to her tree*]: When will you ever need a reason to drink?

PETER [*to himself*]: Probably around the time you need a reason to moan. [*To* CAROL] Any post?

CAROL: On the table.

[*He reaches for the post, declaring what each letter is as he discards it.*]

PETER: Bill. [*Throws away.*] Bill. [*Throws away.*] Christmas card from your aul one. [*Throws away.*] Oh. Now this looks more like it, an American stamp, that'll be my boy, Sam. [*He goes to open it and realises it is already opened.*] It's open.

CAROL: He's my son too.

PETER: They're your fucking bills but I never see yeh open them. [*He takes the letter out, pours another drink and relaxes back in the chair, ready to enjoy the read.*] He's doing fine. Says Rita and the kids love Yonkers. See that Carol, Yonkers . . . spoken like a true Yank. Yonkers, no less. Says they've got a swanky apartment in Manhattan. Listen to this, Carol, for an address . . . listen: Lexington and 77th . . . Jeeesus. [*He looks up from the letter.*] Now why can't we have names like that? They have Roosevelt Island with that bronze statue . . . Harlem with all them music joints . . . Broadway with its theatres . . . And what have we got? . . . O'Connell Street with the fucking floozie in the jacuzzi. [*He goes back to reading.*] He got headhunted. Listen . . . he says, 'Don't worry, Pops, that doesn't mean the Indians got me, it means I got offered a job.' [*He laughs heartily, slapping the table with glee.*] Great sense of humour . . . Takes after me for that. Bloomingdale's offered him the top job in their toy department. Are yeh listening? The biggest toy store in the world and my son is head honcho.

CAROL: We have two sons, Peter.

PETER: Yes, well, the least said about that the better. [*He reads to himself again, then starts to laugh.*] He says that things are really busy, despite nine-eleven. [*Looks up from the letter.*] That's the difference between the Yanks and us. If Bin Liner . . .

CAROL: It's Bin Laden.

PETER: That's what I said . . . If Bin Liner had crashed into us, poor old Bertie would have shit his pants. But not the Americans . . . they're fucking great. And I'll tell yeh, Bin Liner was lucky, 'cause Bushie ain't half the president Clinton was. I'm telling yeh, if Clinton was still in, he'd have told them. He'd a reminded them what happened to the last people that started fucking around with the US. Remember the little yellow bastards over in Japan? The US slapped them all over the Pacific and roasted about two million of them in their own back yard.

CAROL: [*Blesses herself.*] God forgive yeh.

PETER: It's true. Sure, the only reason they never killed Saddam Hussein was 'cause they were pissing themselves laughing at the state of his moustache. That's a well-known fact, that is.

[*He folds the letter back into the envelope. He stands and walks towards his wife. He looks at the tree. She stands back, happy with her work.*]

CAROL: Well. What do you think?

PETER: Of what?

CAROL: Of the tree!

PETER: Yeah, it's fine.

CAROL: Oh, well, don't get too excited now, will ya?

PETER: Well, what do yeh want me to say?

CAROL: I've spent the afternoon getting the place decorated and you waltz in here and don't even comment.

PETER: Come on, love . . . decorating a tree? It's not exactly rocket science now, is it?

CAROL: I must remember that for the next time you come in raving about winning at darts.

PETER: Yeh can't win a turkey for tree decorating.

CAROL: Just forget it.

PETER: What are yeh decorating the place for anyway?

CAROL: Oh, did yeh not hear? It's a new idea . . . we're going to celebrate the birth of Jesus. People have only been doing it for the last two thousand years. But I doubt it'll catch on.

PETER: Very fucking funny. [*He walks back to the table and pours another whiskey.*] I meant, why are yeh bothering? There's only the two of us. Sam and his lot aren't able to come home, not with his new job.

CAROL: We have two sons, you know.

PETER: I only have one.

CAROL: [*Comes to the table and holds two fingers up to his face.*] Sam and Luke, two boys.

PETER [*grabbing her fingers and bashing them into the table*]: Don't you fucking dare do that to me.

CAROL: [*Screams in pain.*] Peter, you're breaking me fingers.

PETER: [*Lets go of her fingers and sits looking at the drink in his hand.*] I have one son. [*Carol moves away from him and starts back to her decorations.*] The other one died the day he started pumping that shit into his body, do yeh hear me? [*He stands up and puts on his jacket again. He heads for the door.*] I'm heading for the chipper to get ME dinner.

EXTERNAL. CITY. BRIDGE. SAME TIME.

[*A down-and-out* LUKE KELLY *sits begging in the street. He has a polystyrene cup held out in front of him and mumbles as people walk by.* JOHN *comes up and puts a couple of coins into his cup. He goes to walk by but recognises* LUKE.]

JOHN: Luke, is that you, Luke? Fucking hell, man, I hardly recked you.

LUKE: [*Looks up and recognises* JOHN.] Ah well, shit happens! Look at you, Don One himself.

JOHN: Ah, yeh know the story, yeh just keep going. [*Looks at his watch and begins to wish he hadn't stopped.*] Listen, Luke, I better be going.

LUKE: Getting the pressies, yeh?

JOHN: Yeh, something like that. A pain in the ballox.

LUKE: What?

JOHN: All this Christmas shite.

LUKE: Jaysus, do yeh hear him? And to think yous used to get the best of stuff. 'Member that mountain bike with all the gadgets on it? [*They both smile, remembering.*] And all we got was a smelly racer with no tyres or nothing.

[*They both laugh.*]

JOHN: But at least yours were bought. The Old Bill took ours back on Stephen's Day, and the aul fella spent his holidays in the nick.

LUKE: Maybe, but still we were dead envious.

JOHN: I was the same about you. Your aul one made the best mince pies in town. I used to love going to yours for a bit of grub. I always wondered why you never got any of it into yeh.

LUKE: What do ya mean?

JOHN: I mean, there was never a pick on ya, still isn't.

[*They both laugh.*]

LUKE: [*Sits and contemplates for a minute, while* JOHN *glances again at his watch.*] Ma was . . . is . . . tops. Yeh know, I wish I could get me act together, make her proud. [*Seems away in his thoughts.*] I wish I could hear her singing to me again. Yeh know, she had a special song for us, yeh know, when we were scared or afraid a the dark or just . . . [*Seems caught up in his own world.*]

JOHN [*looking at his watch again*]: Listen man, I better head. Nice talking to yeh.

LUKE [*ignoring him*]: I remember, if I was crying, she'd hold me real tight, so tight I could hardly breathe, but I knew nothing could get to me and she'd let me hold the sleeve of her nightie . . . [JOHN *starts moving away.*] A big coloured sleeve like a rainbow. And she'd start to sing and suddenly everything would seem all right. [LUKE *starts singing to himself*]:

You used to dream yourself away each night
To places that you've never been
On wings made of wishes that you whispered to
  yourself
Back when every night the moon and you would
  sweep away
To places that you . . . .

[TOWNY *comes by. He is in a hurry and has a box in his hand. He bends on his hunkers beside* LUKE. TOWNY *is nervous, his eyes are shooting around the street.*]

TOWNY: Sign a madness.

LUKE: [*Suddenly realises that* JOHN *is gone and* TOWNY *is there. He stops singing.*] What is?

TOWNY: Talking to yerself.

LUKE: I wasn't talking to meself. I was talking to John.

TOWNY: Fuck . . . imaginary friends and all now. You must be hitting the mushrooms, are yeh?

LUKE [*looking disgusted at him*]: It's not all about scoring, yeh know, there is more to life.

TOWNY: [*Laughs.*] 'Course. Why are yeh sittin' there freezing yer arse off? Are yeh collecting for Vincent De Paul?

LUKE: Yeh know what, Towny? I'm beginning teh wonder the same thing meself. I mean, I'm better than this. I'm looking at fuckers walking past me and them in big fancy jobs and I think, I could do that.

TOWNY: Face it, Luke, you're never gonna do anything but sit on yer arse and wait on handouts. I'm not knocking it: Christmas time . . . people feel guilty . . . throw yeh a few bob to make them feel better . . . it's a nice suss.

LUKE: It's a mug's game.

TOWNY: It's life. Yeh can sit there or yeh can be like me. But either way, all you get is only going one place. [*He rubs his arm.*] And we both love it.

LUKE: What about family, friends . . .?

TOWNY: Are you tripping? What about them? Junkies have no family, junkies have no friends. [*He grabs his parcel and splits it open.*] See that? Swiped it from under a Christmas tree. [*We see a child's present.*]

LUKE: A fucking kid's present? It's Christmas, and you rob a kid's toy from under a Christmas tree?

TOWNY: Supply and demand. That's not me point. Guess whose house it was?

LUKE: How the fuck would I know?

TOWNY: Casey's.

217

LUKE: Our Casey's? Jaysus, Towny, yeh don't piss on your own doorstep.

TOWNY: Would ya stop? That community shit is long gone. Doors left open . . . me bollox. All's fair in love and war.

LUKE: Man, the Caseys live two doors up from me.

TOWNY: Wake up, man, smell the roses. We have no neighbours. [*His eye is taken by a passing granny.*] Oh, I like it. Woman with Zimmer frame, clutching handbag . . . my favourite. [*He pushes the toy towards* LUKE.] Mind that, I'll be back in a second.

[*He runs off, leaving* LUKE *with the toy.* LUKE *is deep in thought, and we know he is contemplating all that has gone on.* DRUG-DEALER *and his* MINDER *come strolling up. They stop either side of* LUKE.]

DRUG-DEALER: Well, well, well, if it isn't me old mate LUKEY BABY.

LUKE: I . . . I . . . I was just about to come and see yeh.

DRUG-DEALER: Well, I saved you the trip then, didn't I? So I hope you have something for me. [*He picks up the cup and empties it into his hand.*] Are yeh holding out on me?

[LUKE *starts at his pockets.*]

LUKE: No, no I have it here.

DRUG-DEALER: If you'd like, Hippo here can help yeh. [*The* MINDER *makes towards* LUKE *but stops short.*]

LUKE: NO! I have it here . . . [*He pulls out a load of coins.*] See?

DRUG-DEALER: I won't count it . . . I trust you. [DRUG-DEALER *and his* MINDER *laugh.*] So tell me what would you like. [LUKE *doesn't say anything.*] We've got some nice speed, keep yeh high all Christmas. Bit a coke, uppers, downers. You name it, I got it.

LUKE: No, nothing.

DRUG-DEALER: [*Pretends to bang his ears as though he has trouble hearing.*] Sorry, I didn't quite catch that. I thought you said 'nothing'? [*He nods to* MINDER, *who grabs* LUKE's *jacket.*] Quit pricking around, I'm busy.

LUKE: I don't want anything. I've paid you back, we're quits, and now I'm going clean.

DRUG-DEALER: Oh, I get it, Christmas time, right? You're thinking about your family. Thinking you want to be like the families in the films. All happy and smiling. [*He signals to his* MINDER *to let* LUKE *go.*] Tell yeh what. Did you ever see that picture *Miracle on 34th Street?* It'd bring a tear to a glass eye. Well, I'm gonna have our very own little 'Miracle on O'Connell Street'. [*He nods to his* MINDER.] Give 'im a freebie.

[*The* MINDER *searches his underpants for the gear. Taking it out, he wipes it on* LUKE's *jacket before throwing it in the cup.*]

LUKE: But I . . . I . . . don't want anything.

DRUG-DEALER: Sure you do. See ya after Christmas. We'll be back to business as usual . . . OK?

[*They walk away, leaving* LUKE *with the gear and the toy. He looks from one to the other and we know he is going through hell.* TOWNY *comes back. He is out of breath but carrying nothing.*]

TOWNY: Jaysus, but them aul ones can't half move on their Zimmer frames. [*He stares ahead.*] Silly bitch. Imagine hanging on to her bag for dear life. Probably only three pounds, a bus pass and a remembrance card in it. [*He looks at* LUKE.] I'm gonna have to get going. I need to get something else before I have enough for me gear. Give us the toy, will ya?

LUKE: I'll swap with yeh.

TOWNY: What, what have you got to swap? I don't need a polystyrene cup and you've fuck all else.

[LUKE *holds up the bag of gear.* TOWNY *goes to snatch it away but* LUKE *is quicker.*]

LUKE: Swap.

TOWNY: What do you want that toy for anyway?

LUKE: I'm giving up, Towny. I'm starting again.

TOWNY: You're fucking mad. Ye'll be on the streets again by Stephen's Day.

LUKE: That's not your concern. I want the toy 'cause I'm heading home, and I'm gonna give the toy back on me way.

TOWNY: [*Looks from toy to bag and grabs the bag.*] OK, OK. Deal. Just don't let on where yeh got the toy from, right? [LUKE *rises.*] Are yeh going now? [LUKE *nods.*] Well, can I have yer stuff?

LUKE: Feel free.

[*As* LUKE *walks off,* TOWNY *wraps himself up in a blanket and, placing the sign in front of him, picks up the cup and starts begging.*]

EXTERNAL. NEW YORK STREET. DAY.

[*A busy New York street. The shops are decked with Christmas decorations and snow is piled up on the sidewalks. The streets are packed. Bruce Springsteen's 'Santa Claus is Coming to Town' plays. Santa (it is* SAM KELLY*) walks out, buttoning up his trousers, and continues singing the song to* *himself (out of tune). Everything he does is exaggerated. He bends to pick up his bell. He starts ringing the bell and calling out.*]

SAM: You better watch out, I'm telling you why . . . Merry Christmas, everybody!

[*People pass, looking unimpressed. A* MAN *walks up. He is eating a burger and stops next to* SAM. *As he looks at him he finishes his burger, wipes his hand on a tissue and throws the tissue into* SAM's *red bag.*]

MAN [*as he walks on*]: Happy holiday.

SAM: [*Looks from the man to the bag and back at the man again.*] Yeah, and a happy new year too. [*He bends down to his bag and starts searching in it.*] Yeh motherfucker. [*From the bag,* SAM *pulls a whiskey bottle in a brown paper bag. Because of his intoxicated state, he believes no one can see him 'sneak' a drink. Having taken a swig, he hides the bottle, wipes his mouth, grabs the bell back up and starts his call again.*] Buck a parcel, Santa's very own presents one miserly dollar, while stocks last . . .

[*A* RICH MAN *walks by. He is smoking a huge cigar and looks very well-off. He stands and watches* SAM *going through his routine. To one side,* MR BLOOMINGDALE *and another Santa –* SANTA 2 *– step into view. They watch.*

As SAM *starts singing again, the* RICH MAN *sticks his cigar into his mouth and claps very slowly.* SAM *sticks his hand out for a tip; the* RICH MAN *takes the cigar out of his mouth and taps it into* SAM's *hand. He walks off;* SAM *looks at the ash then does two fingers after him.*]

SAM: Hey, fuck you, Ebenezer. [*Again* SAM *makes for his bag, mumbling to himself as he searches for the whiskey.*] Do they think

I have nothing better to be doing than freezing my butt off here, like some performing monkey?

[*As he drinks from his bottle and complains to himself,* MR BLOOMINGDALE *walks towards him and stands behind him.* SAM *catches a sight of his shoes and his eyes track all the way from his shoes to his face. When he realises it is his manager,* SAM *tries to hide the bottle while talking.*]

SAM: Mr Bloomingdale, how good to see you. I was just saying what a real pleasure it is to be working for a company such as yours, a real pleasure . . .

MR BLOOMINGDALE: [*Stands looking sternly at him. He looks him up and down, then starts walking around him.*] You know, I've worked here in the toy department for the last twenty-five years – took over from my daddy when he retired. I've seen all kinds of Santas come and go. I've seen big Santas, small Santas, black Santas, white Santas, Asian Santas. I've seen Santas with afro hairstyles; in 1979 we even had a Rastafarian Santa. In fact, if my memory serves me well, we had a completely bald Santa once. I've seen Santas with goatee beards, beards made of cotton wool, real beards down to their knees. At Bloomingdale's, we had the first gay Santa, we even had a politically correct GIRL Santa – [*to himself*] admittedly, she looked more manly than most of our Santas. [*To* SAM] But in all those twenty-five years I've never . . . ever . . . seen a Santa quite like you.

SAM [*with a stupid smile on his face*]: Gee, Mister Bloomingdale, I had no idea you felt that way about me, does this mean I get a bonus?

MR BLOOMINGDALE: Bonus? . . . Bonus? You're sacked, do you hear?

SAM: I'm what?

MR BLOOMINGDALE: Sacked, fired, got the big heave-ho, I've given you the elbow, your cards, you're dumped, on the next bus out of here, you no longer work for Bloomingdale's, AM I MAKING MYSELF CLEAR TO YOU?

> [SAM *starts to walk off, stops and comes back towards him.* MR BLOOMINGDALE *shivers and hides behind* SANTA 2.]

MR BLOOMINGDALE: Touch me and I'll sue.

SAM: [*Goes to the Santa bag and takes out his bottle.*] I just forgot my lunch.

> [SAM *walks away again, only to stop again and come back. Again* MR BLOOMINGDALE, *who has come out from behind* SANTA 2, *cowers.* SAM *reaches into the bag and pulls out a full turkey by the neck.*]

SAM: I forgot my dinner too.

> [SAM *strolls away, swinging the turkey. Happy that* SAM's *gone,* BLOOMINGDALE *stands erect and brushes himself down.*]

MR BLOOMINGDALE [*to* SANTA 2]: Well? What are you waiting for . . .? Get to work before you get your cards too.

EXTERNAL. DUBLIN STREET. EVENING.

> [PAULY, TOMMO *and* NUGGET *stand at a street corner. They kick a can around. Eventually* NUGGET *kicks it out in front of a car and the car runs over it.*]

PAULY [*pointing at the can*]: Yeh fucking eejit, look what yeh did.

TOMMO [*pushing* NUGGET]: Yeah, yeh fucking eejit.

NUGGET [*defensive*]: It was a bleedin' accident.

PAULY: You! were a bleeding accident.

TOMMO: Yeah, the best part of you dripped down yer aul one's leg.

[TOMMO *and* PAULY *push* NUGGET *around the place.*]

NUGGET: Will yas fuck off and leave me alone? [*The three stand, bored. Suddenly* NUGGET *starts pointing down the road, he is very excited.*] Jaysus, look at yer one!

[*The other two follow his gaze.*]

TOMMO: Oh, fuck me.

PAULY: Fuck fuck you, I'd rather fuck her.

[*The three watch an attractive woman drawing closer.*]

NUGGET: Fuck her? I'd eat chips out of her knickers . . .

PAULY: And use her belly-button for the salt.

[*They keep watching her.*]

NUGGET: Would yeh . . . say she does it?

PAULY: I'd say she's mad for it.

TOMMO: Gagging.

PAULY: I'd say she's like the Phoenix Park.

TOMMO: Open all hours.

[*She approaches and they start to smarten themselves up.*]

PAULY: Howya, luv?

TOMMO: Are yeh all right, gorgeous?

[*There's no reply. They watch her pass.*]

PAULY: I'd say she's a carpet-muncher.
TOMMO: Deffo. I'd say she buys cucumbers by the dozen.
NUGGET: Still, she's a nice Swiss roll.

[PAULY *and* TOMMO *look at each other.*]

TOMMO [*to* NUGGET]: Swiss roll?
NUGGET: Yeah, nice tight Swiss roll.
PAULY: [*Slaps* NUGGET *on the head.*] What are yeh like? Swiss roll. What do yeh think she is, a fucking cake?
TOMMO: Are yeh into cakes, yeh? [*They laugh.*] I'd say yeh'd get up on a ring doughnut, would yeh?
NUGGET: Fuck off, will yehs, and leave me alone.

[NUGGET *grabs up the can they were kicking and again they stand around bored.*]

PAULY [*to* NUGGET]: Swiss roll, yeh fucking muppet.
NUGGET: I wonder how Jimmy's doing?
PAULY and TOMMO: Yeah.
NUGGET [*laughing*]: 'Member last year? The craic was bleeding great. [*The others laugh.*] 'Member the church was collecting for the homeless . . .?
TOMMO: Ah yeh, and they had the cake stand . . .
PAULY: And Jimmy laced all the cakes with gear.

[*They all break their hearts laughing.*]

TOMMO: And then he put on 'Patricia the Stripper'.
NUGGET: And that young nun started peeling off her habit.

[*They fall around the place laughing.*]

PAULY: And then the time he recorded the lotto, got a ticket and played the tape in Nugget's aul one's gaff, letting on it was a real draw.

TOMMO: And yer aul one gave him fifty quid on the promise of a grand as soon as he got his cheque.

[NUGGET *stops laughing. The other two don't.*]

NUGGET: That wasn't funny. Our lecky was cut off over that.

[*A voice is heard offstage.*]

JIMMY: Don't tell me you lot are still telling the same shite stories.

[*They look around to see* JIMMY *walk on. They go to hug him but he backs away.*]

JIMMY: Careful, watch the threads.

[*The three look at him.*]

TOMMO: Very nice, Jimmy, where'd yeh get them?
JIMMY: Alias Tom's. I see you lot are still fashion victims. Nugget, if yeh wear them trousers for another year they'll be back in fashion.

[PAULY *and* TOMMO *laugh.*]

JIMMY: I don't know what you're laughing at, Pauly, I'm surprised the *Antiques Roadshow* hasn't snapped up that jacket.

[PAULY *stops laughing as* NUGGET *starts.*]

JIMMY: So what does a man have to do to get a drink around here?

[NUGGET *searches his plastic bag and gets a can. He hands it to* JIMMY.]

JIMMY: A can, for fuck sake . . . I've been on me holidays for nearly a year and the best yeh can do is a fucking can?

PAULY: Well, if we'd known, we would have got a bottle of bubbly.

TOMMO [*reaching for the can*]: Well, if yeh don't want it, I'll have it.

JIMMY: [*Snaps it back.*] I never said that. [*He holds the can up.*] A toast . . . to freedom.

ALL: Freedom!

[*They drink.*]

PAULY: So when did yeh get out?

JIMMY: Monday.

ALL THREE: Monday?

TOMMO: You've been out three days and you're only looking us up now?

JIMMY [*holding his crotch*]: I had some business to take care of.

[*They all laugh.*]

PAULY: Was she good?

JIMMY: THEY were brilliant.

NUGGET: They? You said 'they'?

JIMMY: That's right, two little chinkie peaches.

PAULY: I didn't know chinkies were selling their mutton down Ben Burb Street.

JIMMY: Ben Burb Street? Don't tell me you're still lashing

227

those girls out of it, are yeh? I got Ying and Yang out of the golden pages. [*Sings*] Let yer fingers do the walking.

NUGGET: Must a cost a packet.

JIMMY: Five big ones . . . but it was worth every penny, I'm telling yeh. Them Orientals could teach our birds a thing or two. I mean, fuck education, if they knew how to perform like Ying and Yang, they'd never be short of a few bob.

PAULY: How could yeh afford that kind of money?

JIMMY: What did yeh think I was doing in prison, pulling me plum night and day? I was networking, making contacts, getting ready for when I came out. I'm not gonna stand around street corners for the rest of me life.

TOMMO: Hey, neither are we.

JIMMY: No? Well, tell me then, what jobs have yehs done since I've been in? [*The three look at each other.*] I'll tell yehs what you've been at, will I? Kicking cans and talking about pussy. What yeh would and wouldn't do to a girl. And I'd say yehs haven't even had a ride since I went in.

[*The others look from one to the other again.*]

PAULY: We were waiting on you to come out.

JIMMY: What, to ride?

PAULY: No, to do a job.

NUGGET [*puzzled*]: Were we?

TOMMO [*winking*]: Yeah, we didn't want teh do anything until it was the four of us.

JIMMY: Yeah?

PAULY: Yeah, all for one.

ALL THREE [*raising their cans*]: And one for all!

[*JIMMY shakes his head.*]

TOMMO: What's wrong, Jimmy?

JIMMY: What are yis like? The three fucking Musketeers. [*He goes to walk away.*] Later.

[*They surround him.*]

PAULY: Jimmy, don't go.

JIMMY: What's the point in staying? I've moved on . . . but you . . . yeh sad fuckers . . . have stayed the same. [*They all look at each other.*] I'm playing with the big boys now.

TOMMO: We could too.

JIMMY: [*Smirks.*] Could be a job coming up soon.

PAULY: When?

JIMMY: Next Monday.

[*They all look at each other sheepishly.*]

JIMMY: What's up?

TOMMO: Well, Monday, Jimmy, is a bad day. I have the clinic.

JIMMY: Clinic! What clinic?

NUGGET: Phy, Jimmy. We have to be there for the Phy.

JIMMY: So what are yehs, state-funded junkies? Fucking hell, I'll tell yeh what then, Tuesday. Does that suit yehs?

PAULY: Yeh couldn't make it Wednesday, could yeh? It's just that I've the dole on Tuesday.

JIMMY: Christ Almighty. How do you lot hope to be taken seriously? You've got to be ready 24–7.

ALL THREE: We are, Jimmy.

JIMMY: Empty yer pockets.

ALL THREE: What?

JIMMY: Empty yer fucking pockets. Are yehs deaf as well as thick? I want teh see what yehs are carrying.

[*They empty their pockets: three matches, four cigarettes and about one-fifty in change.*]

TOMMO: For fuck sake, Jimmy. The cops'd be on us like a light if they caught us with as much as a penknife.

JIMMY: That's what I mean. You lot think yer tough, but deep down inside yer afraid. [*He pulls a machete from his pocket, along with two Stanley knives.*] What do yeh think they'd say if they caught me with these? How long do ya think they'd lock me up for?

TOMMO: We can do it, we can carry [*turning to the other two*], can't we, boys?

[*NUGGET grabs one of the knives and starts acting like a swordsman. They all laugh. As they play around with the knives, O'HOGAN walks on. He isn't looking at them.*]

JIMMY: Well, well, well, if it isn't Mister O'Hogan himself.

[*The man swings around and recognises him.*]

O'HOGAN: Howya, Jimmy?

JIMMY [*to the others*]: This thing here . . . is one of the screws from my stay inside. He's the one that nicked me on a visit two months back.

[*The others stop playing and move towards him.*]

PAULY: The bastard!

O'HOGAN: Now, Jimmy, we don't want any trouble.

JIMMY: Jaysus, he's not so smart out of the uniform.

[*The others laugh.*]

JIMMY [*circling* O'HOGAN]: Not so tough without yer back up.

O'HOGAN: I was only following orders, Jimmy. I wouldn't recommend doing anything silly here.

JIMMY: You don't have a choice here, you're not the boss any more. This isn't your patch: it's mine. [*To the lads*] Isn't that right, lads?

[*While* JIMMY*'s attention is diverted*, O'HOGAN *makes a run for it.*]

JIMMY [*watching him run*]: OK, boys, now's yer chance to prove you're ready to move into the big league . . . Get the bastard.

[*They all run off after him*, JIMMY *included.*]

INTERNAL. SAM'S FLAT. EVENING.

[SAM, *dressed as Santa, comes into a room. It is a hovel, a dingy bedsit, dark and unwelcoming.*]

SAM: Hi, honey . . . I'm home. [*There is no answer.*] Where are you? [*He throws the turkey onto the table.*] Hey, Rita, I've got the turkey. [*He walks to the tree and places some presents under it.*] And no peeping under the tree. [*Still no response. He walks to the table and sits. He takes a glass and pours himself a drink. He drinks.*] They must be gone window-shopping. [*He gets up and goes to the answering machine. He hits the button and goes back to the table.*]

ANSWERING MACHINE: [*Pub noises can be heard in the background. It is his father.*] Howya, son? I just thought I'd ring you and see how you're doing. I'll ring yeh later when I get home.

SAM: Yeah, Dad, you do that. Give me a buzz when it suits you. I'd hate to take yeh away from your precious drink. [*He pours another drink.*] He must of got the letter about how good I'm doing. Big job, big apartment. Take a look, Dad . . . take a fucking good look. [*He points around the room.*] A fucking kip, a cockroach-infested hole, but I'm your son, Dad, I couldn't let on. I couldn't say times are hard, I couldn't ask for a handout to tide me over. Failure! What was it, Dad, what was it you used to say? 'There's no such thing as failure, only people who don't try hard enough.' Bullshit, Dad. It's all bullshit. [*He swallows hard.*] RITA! Where are you? [*He notices the note on the board. He walks over and picks it up. He studies it and then starts to read.*] Dear Sam, by the time you get this I'll be on a Greyhound bus heading home. [*Looks up from letter.*] WHAT ARE YOU ON ABOUT? . . . THIS IS HOME. [*Back to letter.*] Please don't try to find us, you'll only convince me to come back and I'd end up hating you. As it is, I still love you . . . I just can't bear to live with you any more. The kids need a better start than this. I know you mean well and there aren't many men who, when sacked from a job, would work as a Santa but . . . I can't stand living from hand to mouth. [*Looking up again.*] I TOLD YOU, IT'S JUST A TEMPORARY SETBACK. [*Back to letter.*] I can't stand not having food on the table. You swore we'd have a turkey and presents but they never happened . . . and what's more, they were never going to happen . . . it's dreams, and all your dreams are in a bottle. You don't need me. Once maybe, but not now. You need help, Sam, and me being there stops you looking for it. You can't keep on blaming your father. You are his son but you are a man, and as a man you have to take responsibility. If you love me, you won't follow. You'll let us start afresh. I'll give the kids a big kiss from you and I'll always tell them that you were a good man. Be safe, I love you. Rita. [*He sits alone and stares at the letter.*]

INTERNAL. PETER'S AND CAROL'S SITTING ROOM. EVENING.

It's Christmas, Carol

[PETER *comes in. He is more oiled than before. He doesn't say anything.* CAROL *is sitting. As he throws his coat on the floor, she gets up.*]

CAROL: I'll put the kettle on.

PETER [*sitting*]: Don't bother, it's Christmas, Carol. I'll have a drop. [*He reaches for the bottle. He pours a drink and knocks it back.*] Any calls?

CAROL: No.

PETER: Sam didn't ring?

CAROL: No, neither did Luke.

PETER: I told you, I don't want that . . . that . . .

CAROL: Son. You don't want that son of yours mentioned around this house. Well, I'm sorry for you but I want him talked about.

PETER: He's an embarrassment. A druggie . . .

CAROL: He's our son.

PETER: Only in name. As far as I'm concerned, he died long ago. I only have one son: Sam.

CAROL: And look what you did to him.

[*She realises that she's overstepped the mark.*]

PETER: What do you mean?

CAROL: Nothing.

[*She gets up and walks from the table. He gets up and grabs her, turning her to face him.*]

PETER: What did I do to him?

CAROL: Nothing, forget it.

PETER: No, explain yourself, woman. You were always jealous of me and him.

CAROL: What?

PETER: Oh, yes, you always mollycoddled Luke and look at the state of him. But me, I brought Sam up. I showed him what hard work and determination can do.

CAROL: Oh, and he really thanked you for that, didn't he?

PETER: What do you mean? I gave that boy everything: worked me arse off, overtime, holidays, weekends, I worked them all to get that boy a proper education.

CAROL: And the minute he had it, he was gone. He couldn't stand the pressure. That boy didn't know the meaning of a good time. It was work, work, work.

PETER: Nothing wrong with a good day's work.

CAROL: What about love? Why couldn't you just love him? Why, for once, couldn't you just tell him how proud you were?

PETER: Oh, yeah, Luke turned out great didn't he, with all that LOVE?

CAROL: Luke couldn't stand the atmosphere here. You and your bullying pushed them both away.

PETER: How dare you? [*He raises his hand.*]

CAROL: Go on, go on, hit me. That's your answer to everything. HIT ME. After all, that's how you've been king of your castle for all these years. HIT ME like you hit us all. [*He moves away and sits.*] The big man with his fists of steel. I should have stopped you years ago. I should have stood up to you, but I was too scared. I thought you'd leave me. Imagine, I let you make my life and my children's lives a misery 'cause I was scared to be on my own. Well, not any more. [*She gets her coat, and he stands in front of the door.*]

PETER: Where are you going?

CAROL: I'm going to bring my son home.

PETER: I won't let you.

CAROL: You can't stop me. [*He hits her. She falls to the floor and looks up.*] You'll have to do a hell of a lot better than that.

234

'Cause if I have as much as one breath in my body, I'm getting him.

[*They stare at each other. He moves from the door and falls to the table, crying. She walks out.*]

EXTERNAL. STREET. SAME TIME.

[LUKE walks by four stoned-out lads.]

YOUTH: Luke! Over here. [LUKE *looks at them.*] Do yeh want something?
LUKE: Yeh, I do, but I won't find it here.
YOUTH: Where yeh going, man?
LUKE: I'm going home, man, I'm going home.

INTERNAL. SPLIT STAGE. SAME TIME.

[SAMMY *and* PETER *sit in their respective sitting rooms. The two scenes mirror each other. Both are drunk, leaning on their tables with an empty bottle in front of them.* PETER *dials a number and we hear the start of* SAM's *answering machine message.*]

PETER: Sammy? You there, Sam? If you're there, please pick up, son, I need you.

[SAM *doesn't pick up.*]

EXTERNAL. DUBLIN STREET. SAME TIME.

[*The gang arrive in a hurry but can't spot* O'HOGAN *anywhere.*]

JIMMY: I could've sworn he came down here.

[*They look around frantically.*]

TOMMO [*to* NUGGET]: That's your fault. [*He hits* NUGGET.] If you weren't so slow, we'd have caught him.

PAULY: [*Hits* NUGGET *too.*] Yeah.

JIMMY: Will yeh give it a rest and look for the fucker?

[*They search again without luck.* JIMMY *is frantic, the others less so.* PAULY *gives up and goes to hand his knife back to* JIMMY.]

PAULY: Pity that, would've been nice to have seen some action.

TOMMO [*handing him his knife too*]: Yeh, fucking shame. If we'd have got him, we'd have . . .

JIMMY: Ye'd have done nothing. Yeh'd have shit a brick . . .

NUGGET: No, no, honest, Jimmy, we were up for it.

JIMMY: Like fuck, yeh were.

PAULY: Listen, Jimmy, there's nothing we can do about it. We gave chase, he got away, end of story.

TOMMO: But if we had have got him . . .

PAULY: He'd have been one dead fucker . . .

TOMMO: We'd have slit him from ear to ear.

PAULY: Like a little pig.

[NUGGET *starts running around the place like a pig. They laugh but* JIMMY *doesn't.*]

JIMMY: OK . . . Prove it.

PAULY: What?

TOMMO: How?

[JIMMY *hands them all their knives back.*]

JIMMY: Next person that passes, no matter who, we do. Agreed? [*They look from one to the other.*] I said AGREED?

[*They nod. They stand in silence and start kicking a can around again.* JIMMY *looks up and nudges* PAULY. LUKE *approaches.*

They continue playing. LUKE *walks between them, nodding to them. When he is in the middle, they attack. He falls to the ground, blood spurting from him. It is a frenzied attack. Suddenly* NUGGET *looks up and sees someone approaching.*]

NUGGET: Sketch!

[*They run away. As they do, they bump into* CAROL.]

CAROL [*shouting after them*]: Watch where you're going! [*She stands watching them.*] Bloody pups. [*She turns to see a body on the ground.*] Oh my God. [*She looks around for help.*] Someone call the ambulance. [*She rushes to the body and, turning it, realises it is* LUKE.]

CAROL: Luke!

LUKE [*very weak*]: Ma, I was coming to see yeh.

CAROL: Oh, Luke, what have they done to yeh?

LUKE: It hurts, Ma.

CAROL: Shush, shush, Luke, the ambulance will be here any minute. [*She looks frantically around.*] For God sake, will someone phone 999?

LUKE: Ma, Ma, I'm sorry for all . . .

CAROL [*rubbing his hair*]: I know you are. Now not another word, do you hear?

LUKE: Ma, Ma, do yeh remember our song? Will yeh sing it?

CAROL: [*Laughs.*] God, it's years since I sang that.

LUKE: Please, Ma, sing it.

CAROL: Sure, I don't even remember the words.
LUKE: [*Sings*] You used to dream yourself away . . .

[*He coughs and grabs onto her sleeve. She holds him closer and, mopping his brow, starts to sing.*]

CAROL: . . . each night.
   To places that you've never been
   On wings made of wishes that you whispered to yourself
   Back when every night the moon and you would sweep
        away
   To places that you knew you would never get the blues.

[*She looks down and sees he is dead. She falls onto him, crying. The music starts and we hear the words of the song played out as she sobs.*]

SONG: Now whiskey gives you wings to carry each one of
        your dreams
   And the moon does not belong to you
   But I believe that your heart keeps young dreams
   Well, I've been told to keep from ever growing old
   And a heart that has been broken will be stronger when it
        mends
   Don't let the blues stop singing
   Darling, you only got a broken wing
   Hey, you just hang on to my rainbow
   Hang on to my rainbow
   Hang on to my rainbow sleeves

[*The lights dim and a moon shape lights up for a second before going out.*]

CURTAIN.

Leabharlanna Poiblí Chathair Bhaile Átha Cliath
Dublin City Public Libraries